RAMBAN
COMMENTARY ON THE TORAH
פירוש הרמב"ן על התורה

BAMIDBAR

DEVARIM

—⸺◦⟨◉⟩◦⸺—

Selected portions of Nachmanides

Annotated and
Translated
by
Rabbi Avraham Yaakov Finkel

YESHIVATH BETH MOSHE
SCRANTON, PA.

ומשימים חתיכות במקומות שחסרו הרבה, או שיכולים ליטול
חתיכות להוסיף עליהם במקום שנחסרו במיעוט לעשות וזהו על פי
וכו'.] ומה שמדמה הזהר מצוות התורה ללבושי מלכות מצינו גם
בזכריה (פרק ג) ויהושע היה לבש בגדים צואים ועמד לפני המלאך
יען ויאמר אל העמדים לפניו לאמר הסירו הבגדים הצאים מעליו
ויאמר אליו ראה העברתי מעליך עונך והלבש אתך מחלצות.
וביאורו דמצוות ומעשים טובים הם הלבושים שמתלבש האדם
בעולם הבא, והם הלבושים שבהם יבא לפני ממ"ה הקב"ה. ומה
שיהושע כה"ג היה לבוש בגדים צואים הוא מפני שהיה פגם במעשיו
כמבואר בחז"ל הובא ברש"י זכריה פרק ג (ג) לבוש בגדים צואים –
כתרגומו הוו ליה בנין דנסבין להון נשין דלא כשרין לכהונתא והיה
נענש הוא על שלא מיחה בידם: (ד) הסירו הבגדים הצואים מעליו –
יבדילו בניו את נשותיהם וימחול לו: הרי מבואר דמעשי מצוות הם
הלבושים בעוה"ב. והקב"ה הבטיח אותנו שיסייע לבא לפניו
בלבושים שלמים. ומבאר הזהר דהפסוק על פי התורה וכו' מדבר על
כח חז"ל לבאר מצוות התורה, שיש הרבה מצוות בתורה שבכתב
ואפי' בדברי המשנה שצריכים הוספה כדי שיהיו שלמים. ועוד נראה
שנכלל בזה הבטחה על כל הדורות. שיש דורות שהם כשרים
במעשיהם ואינם תחת השפעת אומות העולם, והם צריכים הוספה
מעט לבאר להם כוונת התורה ויש דורות שחסרו להם כמה עיקרים,
וגדולי הדור מלמדים להם הדרך האמיתי, עד שיכינו להם לבוש
מלכות כראוי.

וכמו שבלבוש יש לבוש שמכסה כל גופו ויש שחסר בכמותו
שאינו מכסה כל גופו וכן יש חיסרון באיכות הלבוש, שיש העשוי
ממשי ויש מדברים פחותים, כמו כן במצוות אם יחסרו במעשה או
בכונה, הלבוש שנתהווה ממעשי המצוה חסר בכמותו, ואפילו אם
יעשה המעשה בשלימותו ובכונה מ"מ לפעמים יש חסרון באיכות
הכונה, ואיכות הכונה פועל באיכות הלבוש. הרמב"ן בפירושו פירש
הרבה מצות והועיל לנו בכמות ועוד פירש לנו הרבה באיכות
הכונה, כדי שנזכה ללבוש יקר, ועל ידי זה נהיה ראוים לבא לפני
ממ"ה הקב"ה.

הקדמה
מראש הישיבה
מורינו הרב יעקב שניידמאן שליט"א

בגמר ההוצאה של ליקוטי מאמרי הרמב"ן על חומש, עלינו
להכיר חסד הבורא עולם עם כלל ישראל, ששלח לנו הרמב"ן להאיר
עינינו בפירושיו על התורה. הקב"ה משגיח על כלל ישראל להעמיד
בכל דור ודור אנשים גדולים שמורים ומלמדים דרך ה', כדי שנוכל
לקיים ונסבול עול הגלות, ועוד יותר שנוכל לעלות על ידיהם
למדרגה גבוהה של התקשרות לבורא עולם. והוא בכלל מה שדרשו
חז"ל על הפסוק (דברים פרק יז) ובאת אל הכהנים הלוים ואל השפט
אשר יהיה בימים ההם ודרשת והגידו לך את דבר המשפט על פי
התורה אשר יורוך ועל המשפט אשר יאמרו לך תעשה ופירשו חז"ל
וכי יש אדם שהולך לבית דין שאינו בימיו. אלא ללמדך אין לך
לדרוש אלא בית דין של אותה שעה. וביארו שהקב"ה מסייע לב"ד
שבכל דור להורות האמת ואפילו אם אין הב"ד במדרגת דור העבר.
ובכלל הבטחה זו יש סייעתא דשמיא שנכיר בלי ספק מי הם
המנהיגים וגדולי המורים שהם במדרגה עליונה. וברעיא מהימנא על
הפסוק על פי התורה אשר יורוך מבאר, וז"ל הדא הוא דכתיב
(דברים יז) על פי התורה אשר יורוך, לאומן דחתך מאני לבושין
דמלכותא ועבד מנהון חתיכן סגיאין אינון דידעין אתרין דחסרין אלין
חתיכות או אלין דמשתארין אינון מתקנין אינון לבושין ושוין אינון
חתיכות דאתוספן באתר דמעוטין וחתיכות דאינון מעטין מוסיפין
עלייהו והאי איהו על פי התורה אשר יורוך, [זהו שכתוב על פי
התורה אשר יורוך, משל לאומן שחתך מה שנארג והכין בשביל
לבושים למלכות, ועשה מהם הרבה חתיכות, אותם שיודעים מה
מקומות בבגד המלכות שחסרו מיעוט חתיכות, או שמבינים מה
שצריך להוסיף על בגד שחסר הרבה, יכולים לתקן הלבושים,

CONTENTS OF MAJOR THEMES

SUMMARY OF
RABBI YAAKOV SCHNAIDMAN'S
PROLOGUE

Upon the completion of the "Selected portions of the Ramban on the Torah", we thank Hashem for his kindness towards the B'nei Yisrael, for giving us the Ramban, who illuminated our eyes with his explanations to the Torah. Hashem looks after us by sending great people in each generation who teach the path of Hashem, enabling us to exist and to bear the yoke of our exile. They also help us rise spiritually so we can connect with the Almighty.

This is included in the verse, *"And you shall come to the Kohanim the Levi'im and to the judges that will be in that time. You shall ask of them and they will tell you the ruling. Act according to the Torah that they teach you and the ruling they tell you"* (Devarim 17: 9,11). From the words "in that time", our sages derive that one must always follow the ruling of the sages of his time, for there is special Divine guidance that enables sages of each generation to teach the truth even if they are not of the same caliber as sages from preceding generations. The ability to discern who are the great men of the generation is included in this Divine guidance.

The Zohar, expounding on the verse "Act according to the Torah that they teach you", compares the leaders of each genera-

---

Rabbi Yaakov Schnaidman is the Rosh Yeshivah of Yeshivath Beth Moshe — Scranton, Pennsylvania.

tion to a tailor who cuts pieces of cloth for royal clothing. Only one who recognizes where something is missing and where each piece belongs can construct the royal garments. We find in Zechariah as well that the mitzvos of the Torah are compared to clothing. As it says, *And Yehoshua was wearing soiled clothing and he stood before the angel. And he answered and said to those standing before him saying, "Remove the soiled garments from him," and he said to him, "See I have removed your sin from you and have clothed you in clean wraps." (Zechariah 3:3,4)*. Our sages teach us that the soiled clothing refers to sins. Thus we understand that the performance of mitzvos are our clothing for the World to Come.

The Zohar is telling us that the sages teach us how to perform the mitzvos to perfection, for the written commandments and even the oral tradition need to be expounded upon in order to be performed properly. In fact it seems that included in this verse is that the sages of each generation must address the needs of their time, explaining the mitzvos and bringing out the truth so we can merit to have the proper royal garments.

Clothing must be the proper size; if it is too short, part of the body will remain uncovered. A garment can also be made of different materials, with the more refined the material the better the garment. So too, if one does not perform mitzvos properly, or performs them without intent, the "garments" produced by these actions will not be the proper size. Even if one acts properly, and with intention, the better one understands the concepts and meanings behind the mitzvos the more refined will be the material of his "garments".

The Ramban with his commentary has helped us in the performance of many mitzvos, and with his explanations of the underlying reasons for the mitzvos has helped us to acquire "royal garments" which will make us worthy of coming before Hashem the King of kings.

TRANSLATOR'S INTRODUCTION

—=◉=—

This volume which covers the Ramban's commentary on *Sefer Bamidbar* and *Devarim* is the final volume in the series of selections of the Ramban's *Peirush al HaTorah*.

At the outset of *Sefer Bamidbar* the Ramban notes several striking parallels between the *Mishkan* and the Revelation at Sinai, suggesting that the *Mishkan,* and later the *Beis Hamikdash,* were to serve as a permanent dwelling place for the *Shechinah* that rested on Yisrael at Sinai.

In *parashas Behaalosecha* we learn how Aharon's lighting of the Menorah in the *Mishkan* foreshadows the miracle of Chanukah which happened to Aharon's descendant—Mattisyahu the *Kohen Gadol* and the Chashmona'im—at the rededication of the Second Beis Hamikdash.

Moshe's strategy of conquering Eretz Yisrael is the topic of an extensive commentary which deals also with the question as to what was the sin of the spies. After all, they truthfully reported what they had seen. In a thorough analysis of the text the Ramban exposes their evil intent.

The commentary regarding Bilam's donkey leads to an enlightening discussion on the nature of angels, black magic, and the difference between Moshe's prophecy and that of Bilam. The Ramban explains that Bilam's pronouncements refer to events in the distant future of the Jewish people, pointing to final redemption with the coming of Mashiach. As the Ramban phrases it: "The downfall of Edom (Rome) will be by the hand of Mashiach, because our present *galus* is considered Edom's *galus*."

In a very engrossing commentary he explains the puzzling law of the *eidim zomemim*, "the plotting witnesses," which the Gemara calls a *chiddush*, a novel law that defies logic.

Regarding the law by which one must send away a mother bird and only then is one permitted to take the young, and the prohibition against slaughtering a mother animal and its young on the same day, the Ramban says that these commandments are meant to inculcate compassion and good character traits in people, and not, as some think, that G-d Himself has pity on the birds and animals.

Commenting on the *Tochachah*—the series of dreadful curses in *parashas Ki Savo*—the Ramban says that it refers to our *galus* at the hand of "the fourth beast" in the prophecy of Daniel which symbolizes Rome. He summarizes stating that Hashem assured us that we will be completely redeemed from our *galus*.

In his commentary on *parashas Haazinu* the Ramban leaves us the following inspiring message:

"The Song of *Haazinu* does not make the future redemption conditional on repentance, rather it is a declaration predicting that we will transgress, and that in His anger G-d will punish us, but that we will not be totally obliterated. Rather, He will relent and pay back His enemies with His harsh, great, and mighty sword, and will forgive our sins for His name's sake."

The Ramban concludes his monumental and timeless Commentary on the Torah with the following blessing:

May the verse written by Yechezkel be fulfilled:

Then the nations will know that I am Hashem
   Who sanctifies Yisrael,
When My sanctuary will be among them forever (37:28)
Blessed be Hashem the G-d of Yisrael forever,
From this world to the World to Come You are G-d.
Amen and Amen
May this *berachah* come true, speedily in our days.

AVRAHAM YAAKOV FINKEL
Kislev, 5766

BAMIDBAR

DEVARIM

ספר במדבר

An Overview

═══◉═══

Parallels Between the Tent of Meeting and the Revelation at Sinai

After delineating the laws of the offerings in *sefer Vayikra*, the Torah expounds upon the commandments B'nei Yisrael were given concerning the Tent of Meeting. Previously Hashem warned them against defiling the Sanctuary and its holy things; this mitzvah applies at all times. Now He commanded them to set a boundary around the Tabernacle while it stood in the wilderness, just as He had commanded to set a boundary around Mount Sinai while the glory of the *Shechinah* rested on it (*Shemos* 19:12). This mitzvah [only applies for a specific time]. He also commanded here [in *Sefer Bamidbar*], *Any non-Levite who comes close shall die* (*Bamidbar* 1:51), just as He said [at Mount Sinai], *Set a boundary for the people [around the mountain], and tell them to be careful not to climb the mountain, or even to touch its edge. Anyone touching the mountain will be put to death* (*Shemos* 19:12.13).

Similarly, He cautioned here [in *Sefer Bamidbar*], *[The Kehosites] will then not come and see the sacred [furnishings] being packed, and they will not die* (*Bamidbar* 4:20), which parallels the warning [at Sinai], *that they must not cross the boundary in order to see the Divine, because this will cause many to die* (*Shemos* 19:21).

In the same vein, here [in *Sefer Bamidbar,*] He commanded, *Let them be entrusted with responsibility for the Sanctuary and the altar, so that there not be any more Divine wrath directed at B'nei Yisrael* (*Bamidbar* 18:5), just as He instructed [in connection with the Revelation at Sinai], *The kohanim who [usually] come near the Divine must also sanctify themselves, or else Hashem will send destruction among them . . . But the kohanim and the [other] people must not violate the boundary to go up to the Divine, or else Hashem will send destruction among them* (*Shemos* 19:22-24).

Thus Hashem commanded in *Sefer Bamidbar:* Who must guard the Tabernacle and its furnishings; how [the people] must camp around the Tabernacle; that the people must stand at a distance [from the Tabernacle]; how the *kohanim* who come near the Divine, must conduct themselves when [the Tabernacle] is at rest, and when it is being carried [on their journeys]; and how they must guard it. This was a sign of honor and distinction for the Tabernacle, as the Midrash says: One cannot compare a royal palace that is safeguarded to one that is not safeguarded.

SUMMARY

The entire book [of *Bamidbar*] deals only with mitzvos which applied during the time B'nei Yisrael dwelled in the wilderness. It also describes the miracles that happened to them, to relate the wondrous deeds Hashem performed for them. The book also tells us that Hashem began to crush Yisrael's enemies by the sword, and gives His instructions on how the Land should be divided. There are no commandments in this book which are binding for all time, except for a few commandments about offerings. They were started in *Sefer Vayikra,* but since they were not fully explained there, they are finished in this book.[1]

---

[1] The *sefer Uvacharta Bachayim* notes that *sefer Bamidbar* does contains a number of timeless mitzvos, such as *Birchas kohanim, challah, tzitzis, pidyon bechor,* blowing the *shofar* on Rosh Hashanah, and revoking vows. He remains with the question why the Ramban does not mention them.

במדבר

BAMIDBAR

———⸻◉⸻———

THE CENSUS

1:3 You and Aharon shall take a tally of them by their divisions, [counting] every male over twenty years old who is fit for service.

Take a tally of them [*tifkedu osam*] Without exception, the word *pekidah* means remembering and watching over something, as in the verse, *"Hashem* [pakad] *remembered Sarah as He said He would"* (*Bereishis* 21:1). The word *pikadon* ["an article left for safe-keeping"] has the same root [*pakad*] because the guardian watches over the article [entrusted to him]. Hashem commanded that Yisrael be counted with the words, *"tifkedu osam"* hinting that B'nai Yisrael should each give an atonement offering of half-a-shekel, rather than Moshe taking a head count; by [counting] the half-shekels [*tifkedu osam*] the tally of the people will be watched and remembered.

DAVID'S DISASTROUS CENSUS

David [was enticed by an evil impulse to conduct a national census and was punished. He was not punished for failing to

5

count them through an atonement offering, for] it says, *Yo'av reported to the king the [mifkad] number of people that had been counted* (2 *Shemuel* 24:9), meaning he knew the number by counting the atonement offering of a half-shekel that each had given. It is hard to believe that David disregarded the warning[2], against counting without the use of a coin as we are taught, *In this manner they will not be stricken by the plague when they are counted* (*Shemos* 30:12). And if David was mistaken [thinking the command to count by half-shekel was a special one-time ruling which did not apply in his time], why didn't Yo'av [who was the commander of the army of Yisrael and in charge of the census] take the count through half-shekels. We find that the king's command was repugnant to him (1 *Divrei Hayamim* 21:6), for [Yo'av] said to [David], *Why should my lord desire such a thing? Why should this be a source of guilt for Yisrael?* (ibid. v. 3). [If the only sin was counting them without half shekels,] Yo'av could have counted them through half-shekels to avoid the sin.

In my opinion Hashem was angry with David for counting the people of Yisrael unnecessarily, since he was not going to war [and did not need to know the number of men available for military service], and he did not do anything with the men he counted. He counted them merely to exult in ruling over a large number of people. Therefore Yoav said, "*May Hashem your G-d increase the number of the people over and over a hundred times . . . but why should the lord my king desire such a thing?*" (2 *Shmuel* 24: 3).

In *Bemidbar Sinai Rabbah* (2:17), Rabbi Eliezer says in the name of Rabbi Yosi ben Zimra: "Whenever Yisrael was counted for a purpose their numbers did not decline; but when they were counted for no purpose their numbers declined. When were they counted for a purpose? In the days of Moshe at the formation of the banners [around the Tabernacle] (*Bamidbar* ch.2), and at the division of the land (*Bamidbar* ch. 26). [When were they counted] needlessly? In the days of David."

---

[2] The Torah ordains that a census should not be taken by body count, rather, each individual should give a coin, and by counting the coins the census takers arrive at the total.

Possibly David ordered every man in Yisrael above the age of thirteen to be counted, since it does not say [in connection with this count], "from twenty years of age and up." Instead, David said: *Go and count Yisrael . . . and bring me information as to their numbers* (1 *Divrei Hayamim* 21:2), and this is why he was punished. For the Torah only allows counting from twenty years of age and up and by means of half-shekels. Since this [prohibition of counting younger then twenty year olds] is not explicitly stated in the verse, David mistakenly thought that *they will not be stricken by the plague* (*Shemos* 30:12) as long as they are counted by the half-shekels which are an atonement [for their soul, and therefore, even thirteen year-olds could be counted by means of half-shekels]. But Yo'av was concerned about [counting those under twenty years of age].

The text itself suggests this, saying, *David did not take a census of those under twenty years of age, for Hashem had promised to make Yisrael as numerous as the stars of heaven. Yo'av the son of Tzeruiah did begin to count them, but did not finish; and wrath struck Yisrael on account of this* (1 *Divrei Hayamim* 27:23,24).[3] The verse indicates that Yo'av's census included those under twenty years of age, causing Hashem's wrath. For Hashem wants to increase the number of Jews making it impossible to count them, as He said, "*Count the stars if you are able to count them. So shall your offspring be!*" (*Bereishis* 15:8).[4]

The verse, *All of Yisrael numbered one million one hundred thousand men—able-bodied fighters* (1 *Divrei Hayamim* 21:5), does not mean they were all warriors [since the count also included thirteen years-olds who are not fit for military service]. It means they were all healthy and robust enough to go to war, implying he did not count the sick, the weak, and the elderly, because "the king's command was repugnant to him." This explanation is fitting.

---

3   This chapter relates that David divided Yisrael into 12 divisions of 24,000 men each. Our verse says that he did not count those under twenty years of age, the implication being that at the census at which he sinned he counted those under twenty years of age.

4   To count the entire population would make it apparent that Yisrael had not been worthy of the blessing.

But according to the *Midrash Aggadah* there was an actual head-count, and both [David and Yo'av] erred.[5] That is why David said to Yo'av, "*Go and count* [meneh] *Yisrael*" (2 *Shmuel* 24:1) [and not, "Go and number [*pekod*] Yisrael."] Then it says, *David reproached himself after having counted* [safer] *the people* (24:10) [implying that he counted by head rather than by half-shekels], for the Torah [which counted through half-shekels] never uses the term *safar* (to count) in reference to people. The expression *be-mispar sheimos*, [*bemispar* from the root *safar*] "by number of the names" [in the count of Moshe] means each person should announce his name[6] when he is counted by means of his atonement gift [of a half-shekel].

REASON FOR THE CENSUS

1:45 **These were all the countings of B'nei Yisrael, according to their fathers' households . . . all those in Yisrael who were able to bear arms.** The Torah mentioned the total count although it had already stated the tally of each tribe, because Moshe and Aharon were commanded to determine the total number of people as well as the number of people in each tribe; that is the way kings conduct a census of their people.

Although it was necessary to separate the people according to their individual tribes to establish the formation of the four banners, I do not understand why Hashem commanded them to know the number of each tribe.

---

5   They mistakenly thought the command of counting by half-shekel was a one-time special decree. Yoav disapproved of David's command because the census had no purpose, or because he was also told to count also men under twenty years of age.

6   The word *mispar* is derived from the root *safar* which means both "to count" and "to tell, to relate."

A Show of G-d's Love

Perhaps Hashem wanted them to realize how kindly He treated them. When their ancestors went down to Egypt they numbered only seventy persons, and now they were as numerous as the sand of the sea. He also counted them after every plague and epidemic[7] to let them know it is He who increases the nation, and *He crushed and His hands heal* (*Iyov* 5:18) [meaning, that at the same time that He strikes He also heals their wounds]. That is why our Rabbis said: Because of His great love for them He counts them every time, to let them know how much kindness He bestows on them.

A Special Merit

[However, this does not explain why they had to announce their names when they were being counted. Therefore, the Ramban continues:] A person, appearing before the great prophet [Moshe] and his saintly brother [Aharon], who identifies himself by name, gains merit and life, because he has entered the assembly of G-d's people being inscribed in the list of the House of Yisrael; and shares in the merit of the community by being included in their numbers. Each person also receives special merit by being counted before Moshe and Aharon, since they look upon each person with favor pleading for mercy on their behalf, [as it says,] *May Hashem, G-d of your fathers, increase your numbers a thousandfold* (*Devarim* 1:11), may He not reduce your numbers, and may the shekels be a redemption for your souls.

Bamidbar Rabbah explains the verse, *By number of the names . . . according to their head-count* (*Bamidbar* 1:18): The Holy One, blessed be He, told Moshe to count each person with respect and

---

7   Referring to the plagues that struck those that made the golden calf and those that followed Baal Pe'or.

dignity. "Do not say to the head of the family: 'How many are there in your family? How many sons do you have?'" Rather they shall pass before you with awe and dignity, and you will count them. Thus it says, *By number of the names, from twenty years of age and up, according to their head-count* (1:18).

PREPARING FOR WAR

The census may have been taken in preparation for a military campaign, as governments do, for they were about enter Eretz Yisrael, engaging in war against the Amorite kings on the eastern bank of the Yarden and the seven nations [inside Eretz Yisrael], as Moshe said, *We are now on our way to the place that Hashem promised to give us* (*Bamidbar* 10:29). Therefore, Moshe and the leaders of the tribes needed to know the number of people fit for military service, as well as the numbers of each tribe, to give them the correct assignment as they engaged in war. For the Torah does not rely on the miracle of one man pursuing a thousand. This is the intent of the phrase, *everyone fit for military service in Yisrael,* for the census was taken to determine the number of men fit for military service.

Furthermore, Moshe and the leaders, distributing the Land according to their numbers, needed to know how many parts of the conquered Land to allocate to them. For if not for the sin of the spies, they would have entered the Land immediately.

WHY THE TRIBE OF LEVI WAS THE SMALLEST

3:14 **Hashem spoke to Moshe in the Sinai Desert**—The count of the tribe of Levi differed from the other tribes, for even though the Levites were counted from the age of one month and up (3:15) [in contrast to the rest of B'nai Yisrael who were counted from twenty years and up] they numbered only 22,000 (3:39). When they were counted [later] from the age of thirty years and up there were only 8,000 [actually 8,580] (4:48). Thus, their number from twenty years old and up does not reach even half the number of the smallest of the other tribes of Yisrael.[8] They did not yet carry the Ark, so one cannot say the reason [for their small number] was because they suffered casualties due to the sanctity [of the Ark].[9] It is astonishing that G-d's servants and His devout ones should not be blessed like the rest of the people!

I think [their small number] relates to the *Midrash* saying that the tribe of Levi was not enslaved in Egypt and did not have to do harsh labor. By contrast, [the other tribes of] B'nei Yisrael were made miserable with harsh labor in order to reduce their number. To reverse the decree of the Egyptians, the Holy One, blessed be He, increased them,[10] as it says, *The More [the Egyptians] oppressed them, the more [B'nei Yisrael] proliferated* (*Shemos* 1:12). Similarly, with regard to the decree, *If the infant is a boy, kill it* (1:16), it says—*The people increased and became very numerous* (1:20). For the Holy One, blessed be He, said: "We will see whose word will be fulfilled—Mine or theirs." However the tribe of Levi [which was not threatened with decimation] multiplied in a normal way, and therefore did not become as numerous as the other tribes.

Perhaps Yaakov's anger with Shimon and Levi [who killed the males of Shechem to avenge the rape of Dinah[11]] caused their small number. For the tribe of Shimon which now had a large population [of 59,300] was reduced by the plague and by the time they entered Eretz Yisrael they had shrunk to 22,200 (*Bamidbar* 26:14). [Hashem did not want] Levi, the tribe of His devout ones, to diminish through the plague, therefore their number was small from the start.

---

[8] The smallest tribe, Menasheh, from the age of twenty and up numbered 32,200 (1:55).

[9] If the Levites touched the sacred objects, they would be subject to Heavenly death penalty. They were forbidden to gaze on them in their uncovered state, nor were they permitted to touch the Ark even when they were carrying it. It was to be borne only by means of its staves lest they die (Rashi on *Bamidbar* 4:15, Ibn Ezra on 4:20).

[10] They gave birth to sextuplets (*Berachos* 63b).

[11] *Bereishis* 34 (25-30).

נ ש א
NASO

———•○•———

[**B**y Torah law, if someone warned his wife not to seclude herself with a man but she disregards his warning, she becomes a suspected adulteress. In this portion, the Torah tells her husband to bring her to the Bais Hamikdash to determine if she is guilty or innocent. After a lengthy process she is given the Sotah waters to drink. If she is guilty she immediately swells and dies; if she is innocent she will conceive a child.]

THE BITTER WATERS

5:20,21 **But if you have committed adultery**—There is not a single law of the Torah based on a miracle, except this matter [i.e., the test of the bitter waters]. This enduring wonder happens in Yisrael when the majority of the people abide by the will of G-d. For the sake of [Yisrael's] righteousness Hashem desired to deter the women from emulating the immorality of the other nations, cleansing Yisrael from illegitimate offspring, so they remain worthy of having the Divine Presence dwell among them. However, the water's effectiveness stopped when the people became corrupted with immorality, as it says in the *Mishnah* (Sotah 47a): When adulterers increased [in the time of the second Beis Hamikdash] the ceremony of the bitter water was discontinued, for [the bitter waters do not have an effect on the suspected adulteress if her husband is not free from guilt], as it says, *I will not punish your daughters [through the bitter waters] when they commit harlotry, [nor] your daughters-in-law for committing adultery, for [the men] are secluded with harlots and sacrifice with prostitutes. A people that does not understand will stumble* (*Hoshea* 4:14).

This verse does not imply that adulterous women are free from guilt when their husbands engage in adultery; it only means this great miracle will not be done for them, since it was done [to preserve] their honor so B'nai Yisrael could be a holy people. Once they did not understand and desire this goodness, [it was taken from them.] Therefore the verse ends, *A people that does not understand will stumble,* meaning: they will stumble through their foolishness . . .

To sum it up, the waters of the *sotah* was a great miracle and honor for Yisrael.

בהעלתך

Beha'alosecha

———◆———

Why Aharon Was Disheartened

8:2 When you kindle the lamps. Why is the section regarding the Menorah placed immediately after the dedication offerings of the tribal leaders? Aharon was chagrined because neither he nor his tribe had a role in the dedication. But the Holy One, blessed be He, said to him: "By your life! Your service is greater than theirs, for you will prepare and kindle the Menorah every morning and evening." This is Rashi's commentary citing *Midrash Tanchuma*.

Why did G-d comfort Aharon by mentioning [the task of] kindling the Menorah rather than [his assignment of] burning the incense every morning and evening for which the Torah praises him, as it says, *[The kohanim] shall place incense in Your presence* (*Devarim* 33:10). Or [Hashem could have comforted him] by mentioning all the offerings [brought by the kohanim], the priestly meal-offering which the *Kohen Gadol* brings every day, or the service of Yom Kippur which is only valid when done by Aharon, in the Holy of Holies [on Yom Kippur], highlighting that he is Hashem's holy one who stands in His Sanctuary to serve Him and bless His name, and that his entire tribe performs the service to our G-d.

Furthermore, why was Aharon dismayed [at seeing the offerings of the tribal leaders]? After all, his dedication offering was much greater than theirs, for he offered many sacrifices during all [seven] days of the inauguration of the kohanim! The answer cannot be that these offerings were required, and he wished to bring a free-will offering for the dedication of the Altar, as the leaders of the tribes did, because the lighting of the Menorah with which Hashem comforted him was also a required duty.

FORESHADOWING OF CHANUKAH

However, the *Midrash Tanchuma* alludes to the dedication of the Menorah during the time of the second Beis Hamikdash through Aharon and his sons, that is to say, through [Mattisyahu] the Chashmona'i Kohen Gadol and his sons [which we celebrate on Chanukah]. In *Megillas Sesarim*, Rabbeinu Nissim, says: When the [leaders of] the twelve tribes brought the dedication offerings, and the tribe of Levi did not, the Holy One, blessed be He, said to Moshe: Tell Aharon and his sons: "There is another dedication involving the lighting of the lamps, when I will perform wonders and salvation for Yisrael through your sons, and a dedication will be named after them, namely 'the Chanukah of the sons of the Chashmona'im.'" Therefore [the lighting of the Menorah] was placed after the dedication of the Altar. End of Rabbeinu Nissim's commentary.

The *Midrash Yelamdeinu* (*Tanchuma Yashan*) and the *Midrash Rabbah* [on this verse] offer the following commentary: The Holy One, blessed be He, said to Moshe: "Tell Aharon: 'Do not be afraid. You are singled out for greater things. The offerings are brought only when the Beis Hamikdash is standing, but the lamps illuminate the Menorah forever. And the blessings I have given you to bless My children with, will endure for all time.'"

However, now the Beis Hamikdash is destroyed and the offerings cannot be brought, nor can the Menorah be lit, [so why does the Midrash say the lights of the Menorah will shine forever?]

Therefore we conclude that these Midrashim allude to the kindling of the Chanukah Menorah at the renewal of the Altar by the kohanim of the Chashmona'im dynasty, which continues to be observed even after the destruction of the Beis Hamikdash. So too, the *Birchas Kohanim* (priestly blessing, *Bamidbar* 6:24-26) which precedes the chapter of the dedication offerings of the tribal leaders continues forever. These Midrashim explain that the dedication offerings of the tribal leaders was placed between *Birchas Kohanim* and the lighting of the Menorah in honor of Aharon who was not included in those [offerings].

THE SIGNIFICANCE OF THE NUMBER SEVENTY

11:16 Hashem said to Moshe: "Assemble seventy of Yisrael's elders"

Our Rabbis tell us that there are seventy nations speaking seventy different languages, each with its own celestial constellation and heavenly prince [guardian angel] above it, as it says, *and the heavenly prince of Persia* (*Daniel* 10:13), and, *Behold—the heavenly prince of Greece approaches* (*Daniel* 10:20). It also says, *Hashem will deal with the hosts of heaven in heaven* (*Yeshayah* 24:21). The Gemara explains that the seventy bulls [offered during the seven days of Sukkos] symbolize [the seventy national groups of the world]. And in *Pirkei d'Rabbi Eliezer* (ch. 24) it says [referring to those who built the Tower of Babel]: The Holy One, blessed be He, said to the seventy angels surrounding the Throne of Glory: "*Come let us descend and confuse their speech*" (*Bereishis* 10:7). That is also why the number of individuals [in Yaakov's family] entering Egypt was seventy.[12]

---

12 Perhaps in order that the *Shechinah* should rest on them as It rested on the guardian angels of the seventy nations.

CORRELATIONS BETWEEN HEAVEN AND EARTH

Hashem commanded that Yisrael have seventy judges since the number seventy includes all [possible] opinions [in any case that may come up]. Encompassing all powers, nothing will be too baffling for the judges. At the Giving of the Torah it also says, *Go up to Hashem along with Aharon, Nadav and Avihu, and seventy elders of Yisrael* (*Shemos* 24:1). A group composed of the perfect number [of seventy men] is worthy of having the glory of the *Shechinah* rest on it, just as the *Shechinah* rests on the camp [of angels] in Heaven, for Yisrael is Hashem's army on earth. [The correlation between the heavenly and earthly realm is evident in] the Ark and its cover and the Tabernacle which were made in the likeness of the heavenly beings that serve G-d Above. Similarly, the four banners [of the tribes] were arranged in the image of the Divine Chariot which Yechezkel saw in his vision (*Yechezkel* ch. 1), so the *Shechinah* should rest on them on earth just as It dwells in Heaven.

Continuing this train of thought, Moshe presiding over the seventy elders, symbolizes Yisrael, "a unique nation on earth" [bringing the total to 71]. Additionally, our Sages received a tradition that every Great Sanhedrin seated in the House of G-d—the place which G-d will choose as the dwelling for His Name—should be composed of seventy judges under the leadership of a chief justice, to comprise a total of seventy-one judges.

[The parallel between Heaven and earth is also seen in] the Ineffable Great Divine Name which has seventy-two letters, corresponding to the [seventy] guardian angels of the nations [in addition to the guardian angel of Yisrael,] and Hashem, the One and Only Master over all [bringing the total to seventy-two].

THE QUAIL

11:4-23 . . . and the Children of Israel wept and said "Who will feed us meat?" . . . And Hashem said to

Moshe . . . tell the people "prepare yourselves for tomorrow
and you shall eat meat . . . you will not eat it for one day . . .
but for a month, until it is coming out of your noses [making
them] nauseated . . . And Moshe said "There are 600,000 people in the nation that I am in its midst, and You say 'I will give
them meat for a month.' Can sheep and cattle be slaughtered
for them and suffice for them? Or if all the fish of the sea will
be gathered for them would it suffice?"

The entire episode is astonishing, as Rabbi Shimon said: [Would
Moshe,] about whom the Torah says, *In My entire house he is the
trusted one* (12:7), say, G-d cannot provide enough for them!
Besides, they had already seen much greater wonders than this!
According to Rabbi Avraham Ibn Ezra, Moshe believed G-d would
only perform a new wonder to substantiate the righteousness of
His prophet [as He did in the case of Korach's rebellion, and would
not create a miracle just to fulfill the people's request for meat].

But I do not think this is correct, because G-d did perform similar miracles when He sent a flock of quail (*Shemos* 16:13), when
water [came out of the rock] (*Shemos* 17:6), and when He sent the
manna (ch. 16); these things were given to them in response to
their complaints [and not to validate a prophet].

WHY MOSHE EXPRESSED SKEPTICISM

The correct interpretation is: Hashem performs signs and miracles for Yisrael out of His kindness, and [the miracles] are
good for Yisrael, for He is good to all, and His mercies are on all
His works. However, when He is angry with those who transgress
His will, [He] punishes them with His wrath and strict justice.
Thus [G-d performs] miracles either to show His compassion and
perfect goodness, or to inflict punishment through His attribute of
justice. When Hashem told Moshe He would fulfill Yisrael's request, and they would eat meat *until it is coming out of [their] noses
making [them] nauseated*, Moshe knew Hashem would not per-

form a miracle to supply them with [naseauting] meat as He did when He gave them the "heavenly grain" [of manna], because the Sages say: "Nothing unclean comes down from heaven." Furthermore, G-d announced the miracles before performing them, as we find: *I will make bread rain down to you from the sky* (*Shemos* 16:4); *I will stand before you there on the rock at Chorev. You must strike the rock, and water will come out of it for the people to drink* (*Shemos* 17:6). Yet here, G-d told Moshe, *Tell the people as follows: Prepare yourselves for tomorrow and you shall eat meat,* without saying [He would give them the meat.] Therefore Moshe realized the meat would not come through a miracle [but by natural means], so he wondered how meat could be had [in the desert] without a miracle, saying, *Even if all the cattle and sheep were slaughtered could there be enough for them? If all the fish of the sea were caught, would it be sufficient?* (11:22).

THE QUAIL CAME BY NATURAL MEANS

Hashem explained that His power is not limited even by the normal order of things. Therefore G-d answered, *You will now see whether or not My word will come to pass,* using the word *hayikrecha* "will come to pass" [which is derived from the word *keri* "coincidence, natural means"]. He said, *Has G-d's hand become short?*, but did not say: "Is anything too wondrous for Me?" since [the quail] did not come through a miracle. And indeed—[the quail came by natural means], for G-d caused an ordinary, normal wind, *which swept quail up from the sea* to start blowing. The wind was neither a very strong west wind nor a strong east wind—as in the case of the miracle [of the parting of the Red Sea]—nor were the quail created now for Yisrael's sake, so there was nothing supernatural [about the arrival of the quail]. Moreover, this had already happened before; the only new aspect was that the quail came in great profusion this time.

שלח לך
SHELACH LECHA

THE SPIES

13:1,2 Hashem spoke to Moshe, saying, Send out men for yourself and let them spy out the land of Canaan, that I give to B'nai Yisrael. One man from each tribe you shall send, every one a leader. Rashi comments: [The phrase, *for yourself* implies:] "according to your judgment." [Hashem said to Moshe:] I am not commanding you [to send the spies]. If you wish, go ahead and send them. [Hashem said this,] because the people said [to Moshe], *Send men ahead of us to explore the land* (*Devarim* 1:22), as it says, *All of you then approached me* (1:22), whereupon, Moshe consulted G-d. Replied G-d: "I told Yisrael [the Land] is good, as it says, *I will bring you out of the wretchedness of Egypt . . . to a land flowing with milk and honey* (*Shemos* 3:17). [Since they doubt My word, I swear] by their lives, I will give them an opportunity to err through the words of the spies, so they will not take possession of the Land". [End of Rashi's commentary based on *Sotah* 34b, *Bamidbar Rabbah*, and *Tanchuma*].

WHAT DID THE SPIES DO WRONG?

One may ask: If [Yisrael sinned by asking to send the spies], Moshe also sinned, for he said, *The idea [of dispatching spies] was good in my eyes* (*Devarim* 1:23). And why did he tell the spies to see what kind of land it is, saying, *Is the inhabited area good or bad?* (13:19), when Hashem already told him that it was *a good and spacious Land* (*Shemos* 3:8)?

What was the spies mistake? After all Moshe told them, *See what kind of land it is. Are the people who live there strong or weak, few or many? Are the cities where they live open or fortified?* (13:18,19). Surely they had to report about the things he ordered them to check out. What was their sin when they told Moshe, *However, the people living in the land are aggressive, and the cities are large and well fortified* (13:28). Should they have brought back a false report?

Do not think their only failing was reporting *it is a land that consumes its inhabitants* (13:32), for even before they said this, Kalev spoke out against their [negative] description [of Eretz Yisrael] (13:30).

Furthermore, it says [in *Devarim* 1:26], *[The people said:] "Our brothers [the spies] took away our courage by telling us that they saw there a race that was larger and taller than we, with great cities fortified to the skies, as well as the children of the giants [Anakim]."* And here [in *Shelach Lecha*] it says, [*The people said:*] *Why is G-d bringing us to this land to die by the sword? Our wives and children will be captives* (*Bamidbar* 14:3). [How can the spies be faulted,] when Moshe himself spoke in the same vein to the children [of the generation of the wilderness], intimidating them with the power of the people, the fortifications of the cities, and the might of the many giants in more frightening terms than spies had reported to their parents, [for Moshe said,] *Listen Yisrael, today you are preparing to cross the Yarden. When you arrive, you will drive out nations greater and more powerful than you, with great cities, fortified to the skies. They are a great nation, as tall as giants. You know that you have heard the expression, "Who can stand up before a giant"* (*Devarim*

9:1,2). If the spies sinned by [reporting these things to the parents,] why did Moshe demoralize the children in the same way?

Additionally, why did Moshe send the spies on this mission? We cannot think if they reported that the Land is good and its population is weak, he would continue; but if they reported that the Land is bad and the people are strong,—he would bring B'nei Yisrael back to Egypt!

MOSHE'S STRATEGIC PLANNING

The explanation is as follows: B'nei Yisrael wished to follow the example of [other nations] invading a foreign country who send out scouts to spy the roads and access ways to the cities. When these lookouts return, they march in front of the army showing them the way, as it says, *Show us the approach to the city* (*Shofetim* 1:24), and advising them about which city to attack first, and from which direction it is easy to conquer the Land. Indeed the Torah says, *Let them bring back a report about the way ahead of us and the cities that we shall encounter* (*Devarim* 1:22), meaning: the cities we will go to first, from there advancing across the country.

This strategy is used by all invading armies. Moshe himself used this tactic, as it says, *Moshe sent out men to reconnoiter Yazer* (*Bamidbar* 21:32), and Yehoshua also, sent out two spies (*Yehoshua* 2:1). Moshe approved [of the proposal to send spies,] because the Torah tells us not to rely on miracles. Instead, it commands those going to war to arm and protect themselves, setting ambushes, as G-d commanded before the battle for the city of Ai (*Yehoshua* 8:2), and in many other places.

Thus Moshe consulted G-d, and He gave permission, saying, "Send out men to explore the Canaanite territory, becoming acquainted with it, and bringing back a report to you; on the basis of their information plan your attack."

INSTRUCTIONS TO THE SPIES

A ccordingly, Moshe told the spies, *Head north to the Negev* (13:17), meaning: "Go to the Negev, getting to know the people who live in this region which faces Yisrael's encampment, and see whether they are strong, in which case [our troops] will be heavily armed, and advance cautiously. Notice if the cities are fortified and the inhabitants are sheltered, in which case we will build siege towers and ramps or perhaps it is better to launch an attack from a different direction." Moshe also instructed them to see if the land is good or bad, [because the spies entered the country at a point near Chevron which is the most rugged part of Eretz Yisrael.] If it is bad, they would conquer other parts first. Even Yehoshua did not conquer all of the land. When Moshe said, *whether the inhabited area is good or bad* (12:19), he referred to the population of the Negev.

Perhaps, Moshe knew the land was fertile and good, for Hashem told him, *I will bring them . . . to a good and spacious land* (*Shemos* 3:8), therefore he told the spies to substantiate and report this, so the people would be encouraged and march joyfully to the land. Therefore he told [the spies], *Take courage, and take some of the fruit of the land* (13:20), so [the people] can see with their own eyes how wonderful the land is.

The distance between Egypt and Chevron is only a seven-day journey, and the Land of Canaan borders close to Egypt, so it is impossible that people living in Egypt did not know whether Canaan is a good or bad land. Moshe's intention [in sending the spies] was to decide which route to use and which cities to capture first, as I explained. But B'nei Yisrael, having been slaves at hard labor in Egypt had no idea of the quality of Eretz Yisrael. Therefore Moshe wanted [the spies] to describe the features of the land in detail to make B'nai Yisrael look forward to going there, since Moshe himself knew [the excellence of] the land.

One Man From Each Tribe

A nalyzing the text, it seems to me that Moshe did *not* consult G-d [whether or not to send spies]. The passage, *Send out men for yourself* (13:1) means: The people decided to send spies. Usually two men were sent [on spying missions] as Yehoshua did (*Yehoshua* 2:1), but G-d who knows the future [and foresaw that the spies would bring back a bad report] told Moshe to send the leader of each tribe. G-d wanted great men to be sent out on Moshe's orders, so they should remember [his instructions] and return to Hashem [with a good report]. And if not, He wanted to punish the entire people equally. *Moshe sent them . . . at Hashem's bidding* (13:3) means: at Hashem's command [the spies] were tribal leaders and heads of B'nei Yisrael.

This appears from the text because G-d did not mention the people's request for spies, nor Moshe's approval of that request. Were that the case, the Torah would have stated, "B'nei Yisrael approached Moshe, saying: 'Let us send men ahead of us . . . and Moshe approved of it.'" Then it would have said, "Hashem spoke to Moshe saying: 'Send out men for yourself, as they have spoken to you, one man for each tribe.'"

Rather: B'nei Yisrael asked Moshe to send spies, and he approved. After that, Hashem spoke to Moshe, *Send out men . . . To explore the land of Canaan that I am about to give to B'nei Yisrael,* speaking about something He had not yet mentioned. [G-d commanded them to send spies, though the people had already decided on their own to send them] because, in His righteousness, G-d wanted the spies to be sent at His command, so all the tribes should be involved in this undertaking, sending their great men, to be saved [from sinning].

VEYACHPERU vs. VEYASURU

It also appears that B'nei Yisrael said, *Let us send men ahead of us,* veyachperu *and let them spy out the land* (*Devarim* 1:22), meaning to scout the routes best suited for conquest. *Veyachperu* is from the root *chafar* ["to dig, to search"] as in, *from there* chafar *he searches for food* (*Iyov* 39:29). The intent of the word, "ahead of us," implies that the people would follow after them, similar to, *The Ark of the covenant traveled three days ahead of them* (10:33). Hashem, however, commanded [not *veyachperu* meaning to search the way for conquest] rather *veyasuru the land of Canaan,* denoting "choosing and scrutinizing an article one is about to buy," [to see the great benefits of the land] as in, *besides [the tax income] of the* me'anshei hatarim[13] *small shopkeepers[14]* (2 *Divrei Hayamim* 9:14). Also, *to the land that* tarti[15] *I had sought out for them* (*Yechezkel* 20:7), and, *In order* lasur[16] *to find for them a place to settle (Bamidbar 10:33).* Therefore, Moshe commanded them to state specifically whether the land is good or bad . . . whether the soil is fertile or lean. This would excite the people about going to the most beautiful land on earth.

The story [of the spies] is related here [in *Shelach lecha*] without specifics, but in *parashas Devarim,* Moshe mentioned everything from the beginning, to let B'nei Yisrael know that they sinned by taking the initiative in making the request [to send spies].

Our Rabbis say they sinned by saying, *Let us send men ahead of us* (*Devarim* 1:22). Having seen Hashem continually save them, they should have followed the Cloud wherever it would take them. Yet Moshe accepted their proposal, to placate them letting them have their way. *I approved of the matter* (*Devarim* 1:23) means: I resigned myself to your evil plan, ordering you to implement it. G-d commanded Moshe to send one man from each tribe, just as

---

13 *hatarim* from the same root as *veyasuru.*
14 Small traders who usually carefully examine an article before buying it.
15 *tarti* from the same root as *veyasuru.*
16 *lasur* related to *veyasuru.*

He said to Shmuel, [when the people demanded that he appoint a king], *Listen to the voice of the people in all that they say to you, for it is not you whom they have rejected, but it is Me whom they have rejected from reigning over them* (1 *Shemuel* 8:7).

HASHEM DID NOT DESIGNATE THE SPIES

The spies were not named by G-d. Instead, He commanded Moshe to send a leader from each tribe. Moshe chose them himself, and they brought evil on themselves. By contrast, [G-d did designate the leaders by name] at the census (1:5-15) and at the parceling out of the Land (34:19-28). For no mishap occurs to those who carry out the command of Hashem, and *One who obeys the commandment will not suffer from evil* (*Koheles* 8:5).

THE KEY WORD *EFES*, "BUT"

13:27,28 **It is indeed flowing with milk and honey . . . But, the people that dwell in the land is powerful.** Since Moshe commanded them to see whether the land is fertile or lean, the spies reported that is was fertile, flowing with milk and honey. He also commanded them to show the fruit so they replied: "*And this is its fruit.*"

They told the truth in this, reporting the things they were commanded [to verify]. Similarly, they gave a factual reply regarding the strength of [the people and] the cities. However by adding the word *efes*, "but" [*But—the people is powerful and the cities are very greatly fortified*], the spies showed their wicked intent denoting that the [conquest] is beyond our reach, and cannot be done under any circumstances, as in, *Ha'efes—Is His kindness ended forever?* (*Tehillim* 77:9), and, *There is none other,* efes *except G-d* (*Yeshayah* 45:14).

Thus the spies reported that the land is fertile, flowing with milk

and honey, but impossible to conquer because the people are powerful and the cities are fortified and very great. What's more, we
saw the children of the giant Anak there.

Kalev tried to quiet the people (13:29), saying, *We must go forth
and occupy the land. We can do it!* (13:30), implying: Although the
people are strong, we will be stronger than them and their fortified
cities.

Then the spies openly declared what they really had in mind, *We
cannot go forward against those people; they are too strong for us!*
(13:31). They meant: Even if the people fought us on the battlefield we could not beat them, surely we will not be able to conquer
their fortified cities. The meaning *go forward against the people* is
similar to [Goliath's statement], *Choose yourselves a man and let
him come forward to me!* (1 *Shemuel* 17:8), signifying fighting in
battle formation.

THE SPIES INCITE THE COMMUNITY

13:32 **They began to speak badly about the land . . . to
B'nei Yisrael.** The spies left Moshe and Aharon and
told people in their tents that *the land consumes its inhabitants*
(13:32). At first they spoke to the people in front of Moshe and
Aharon, saying the land flows with milk and honey, but the people
are strong. Kalev responded, *We must go forth and occupy the land.
We can do it!* (13:30), and the people wavered [between these two
opinions], some with faith in their strength and power, and some
trusting in G-d's help. Then the spies told the people, privately that
the land consumes its inhabitants, until they incited the entire community to complain. Thus the passage, *They returned and made the
entire community complain against [Moshe] by spreading a report
about the land* (14:36).

This happened because the spies, seeing the [Amorite] people
tall as cedars and strong as oaks, were gripped with fear, so they dis-
couraged their brothers. When B'nei Yisrael wondered whether or

not to go forward [to Eretz Yisrael], and Yehoshua and Kalev encouraged them, they spread a false report to completely foil the plan of going forward.

Encouraging Words

14:9 **But don't rebel against Hashem. Don't be afraid of the people in the Land . . . they will be our prey, their shadow [their protection] has left them, and Hashem is with us. Do not fear them.**

[Moshe and Aharon told the people:] "Feeling intimidated by the people dwelling in the Land is an act of rebellion against Hashem. It was not by your own strength that you came out of Egypt. The hand of Hashem performed miracles for you, and He assured you He will drive them out before you. Believe in Him, and you will be successful!"

[They] continued: *Don't be afraid of the people in the Land . . . they will be our prey* (14:9),[17] implying: They will fall before us even by natural means and by the norms of warfare, because they are terrified of us. We will devour them like a slice of bread.

Their Shadow

They have lost their protection, [literally: "their shadow."] Rashi explains: [They lost] their shield and their strength; the righteous ones among them have died. Another explanation: G-d's protection [lit. shadow] has left them.

Rabbi Avraham ibn Ezra explains that *tzillam*, "their shadow" in this context means "their shield and armor" which are a warrior's protection. [Moshe and Aharon] were saying: [The Cannanites] are so terror-stricken, they don't even put on armor, shield, and

---

17   Literally: "They will be our bread."

helmet to protect themselves and fight against us. He explains it correctly.

Possibly, the Torah hints to the well-known fact that on the night of *Hoshana Rabbah* no shadow falls on the head of a person who will die that year. Thus the verse is saying: *"Their shadow has departed from them,* because they have been sentenced to death. *Hashem is with us,* He dwells in our midst performing miracles and wonders for us for all to see, *so don't be afraid!"* (14:9).

Or possibly, "their shadow" hints to the guardian angels [of the Amorite and Canaanite nations], since no nation falls unless its guardian angel falls first, as it says, *It shall be on that day that I will deal with the hosts of heaven in heaven, and with the kings of the earth on the earth* (*Yeshayah* 24:21),[18] and as the Book of Daniel plainly states it (*Daniel* 10:20). Thus this verse says: ["Their shadow," namely,] the power under whose protection the [Canaanite and Emorite] nations live, has left, and Hashem who brought them down is with us; *so don't be afraid.* In the same vein Midrash Shir Hashirim says: *And the shadows flee* (2:17)—these are the princes of the nations and their guardian angels. I mentioned this in other places.[19]

---

[18] The guardian angels of the nations will be eliminated, and their earthly constituencies will follow them into oblivion (Rashi).

[19] Yisro 20:3, Acharei 18:24, Behaaloscha 11:15

קרח
KORACH

———◈———

WHO SHOULD SEPARATE?

16:21 [In the course of the Rebellion of Korach who challenged Moshe's authority, Hashem said] **Separate yourselves from among this community, and I will destroy them in an instant.**

If B'nei Yisrael did not sin and did not rebel against Moshe, why was G-d angry with them, saying, *I will destroy them in an instant?* And, if they did rebel along with Korach and his party, how could Moshe and Aharon pray [in their defense], *If one man sins, shall You direct Divine wrath at the entire community?* (16:22).

RABBEINU CHANANEL'S ANSWER

Rabbeinu Chananel answers, *Separate yourselves from among this community* means the people should separate from Korach's party, *not* that Moshe and Aharon should separate themselves from the community of Yisrael. But Moshe and Aharon [mistakenly] thought G-d wanted them to remove themselves from the community of Yisrael. Therefore they said, *If one man sins, shall You direct Divine wrath at the entire community?* Thereupon G-d immediately informed Moshe that He did not mean to destroy the entire community of Yisrael; only Korach's party [would perish]. He explained: When I said: *Separate yourselves from among this community*, I meant: [B'nei Yisrael should] separate from the dwelling of *Korach, Dasan, and Aviram* (16:24). Hashem told them to separate, so Korach and his party, seeing them go away, would [realize G-d intended to punish them] and repent. [End of Rabbeinu Chananel's commentary].

RAMBAN DISAGREES

But [Rabbeinu Chananel's] explanation is not correct. "The community" in, *Separate yourselves from among this community*, cannot refer to Korach, Dasan, and Aviram because three men are not a community, and B'nei Yisrael were not among them.

Furthermore, [the command, *Separate yourselves* was also given to Aharon] and Aharon was with the group that offered the incense!

Besides, *Separate yourselves* was addressed only to Moshe and Aharon, just as, *Stand clear of this community* (17:9).

Similarly, the phrase, *I will destroy them in an instant* (16:21) refers to a plague which consumes a large population, [thus it cannot refer to Korach, Dasan, and Aviram].

Finally, how can one say that Moshe, G-d forbid, did not understand a prophetic message, misinterpreting its meaning!

RAMBAN'S ANSWER

The following will answer [why G-d was angry with B'nei Yisrael, and if they did rebel, why Moshe and Aharon defended them: When Korach began his uprising against Moshe and Aharon], the people sided with Moshe and Aharon. Then Korach and his party took fire pans with incense, and stood at the entrance of the Tent of Meeting along with Moshe and Aharon. Korach rallied the entire congregation, telling them he was fighting for the dignity of all of them. They assembled, hoping G-d would return the service [of the offerings] to their firstborn, [for the Levites had taken the place of the firstborn (*Bamidbar* 3:45)]. This is implied in the verse, *Korach rallied the whole assembly to the Tent of Meeting* (16:19). Therefore, they all became liable to destruction, because they thought ill of their teacher Moshe, which is like thinking ill of the *Shechinah*. They also disregarded the words of a prophet, which made them liable to death at the hands of Heaven.

But Moshe and Aharon defended them, saying that it was only Korach who actually sinned, seducing them and making them sin. Only Korach should die, in order to publicize his punishment to the people. This is how a defender pleads for mercy [for his client]: he mitigates the sin, blaming the individual who caused it, since he is definitely liable in any event.

David Defends the People

David made a similar plea [when the angel struck the people after he counted them,][20] *Behold! I have sinned and I have transgressed; but these sheep—what have they done? Let Your hand be against me and my father's family* (2 *Shemuel* 24:17). [David blamed himself] even though the punishment [of the plague] came on the people because of their own sin. They should have given half-shekels [to be counted]—according to the interpretation that the punishment came because they took a head count. David did not command them *not* to give half-shekels, since he only wanted to know their number, therefore, they [and David] shared the guilt equally. [Nevertheless, David pleaded that Hashem acquit the people and place the full blame on himself].

---

[20] Counting the people is sinful because it is motivated by a desire to know the military strength of the nation. This leads people to rely on their army instead of trusting in Hashem. The Torah commands that the counting should be done by means of half-shekels so that the reason for the census is fund raising for a mitzvah cause.

Delay in Building the Beis Hamikdash

A ctually, the people were liable to punishment even before the census began, as it says, *The anger of Hashem again flared against Yisrael, and He enticed David because of them* (2 *Shemuel* 24:1) [thus, G-d was angry with Yisrael even before the census]. Rashi comments: "I do not know why G-d was angry with Yisrael." But I think Yisrael was punished because they delayed in building the Beis Hamikdash. The Ark was moved from tent to tent as a stranger in the land, yet no tribe took the initiative, saying: "Let us seek Hashem, and let us build the Beis Hamikdash in honor of His name, in compliance with the command, *Seek to establish His Sanctuary, and come there* (*Devarim* 12:5)." Finally, David made an effort [to build the Beis Hamikdash] long [after becoming king], as it says, *When the king was settled in his palace, and Hashem had granted him safety from all the enemies around him, the king said to the prophet Nasan: "Here I am dwelling in a house of cedar, while the Ark of Hashem abides in a tent"* (2 *Shmuel* 7:1,2).

David Is Prevented From Building the Beis Hamikdah

B ut G-d rebuffed David, saying, *"You have shed much blood and fought great battles, you shall not build a house for My name* (1 *Divrei Hayamim* 22:8). Because of this, the building was further delayed until the reign of King Shlomoh. Had Yisrael really wanted, the Beis Hamikdash could have been built in the days of one of the Judges, or in the days of Shaul, or even in the days of David. For if the tribes of Yisrael had been eager to build the Beis Hamikdash, they—and not David—would have been the builders.

Negligence in Building Beis Hamikdash

But since the people were indifferent and it was David who cared enough to give the impetus and prepare the [financing and the building materials], he would to be the builder. However, because he had an uncompromising personality and was guided by the principle of strict justice, he was not the right person to build the House of Mercy. Therefore due to the negligence of Yisrael, the building of the Beis Hamikdash was delayed throughout his lifetime, and that was the reason for the Divine anger [mentioned in 1 *Shemuel* 24:1]. That is also why the site which Hashem selected to place His Name, was revealed through their punishment and plague. [For G-d showed David the location of the future Beis Hamikdash through the image of an angel holding a drawn sword over Yerushalayim pointing at the threshing floor of Aravnah haYevusi which was the site of the future Beis Hamikdash (*Redak* on 2 *Shmuel* 24:16)].

The text alludes to this, for [Hashem said:] "*I have not dwelled in a house from the day I brought B'nei Yisrael up from Egypt to this day; I have moved about in a tent and a Tabernacle. Wherever I moved about among all B'nei Yisrael, did I say a word to one of the leaders of Yisrael whom I have appointed to shepherd My people Yisrael, saying, 'Why have you not built Me a house of cedar?'*" (2 *Shmuel* 7:6,7). Thus the verse blames Yisrael since the *Shechinah* moved about from tent to tent and from Tabernacle to Tabernacle, and none of the Judges of Yisrael, who were their shepherds, set the matter right.

The verse also says Hashem stayed far away from them, not telling any of them to build the Beis Hamikdash. Only when David took the initiative to build it, did Hashem say, "You have done well by having this in mind, but now I command that it be built by your son Shlomoh, who will be a man of peace."

REMOVE YOURSELVES!

17:10 **Remove yourselves from among this assembly . . .** I do not understand the meaning of this verse nor of its counterpart above, *Separate yourselves from amid this assembly* (16:21). Surely G-d can punish a large crowd with the plague sparing one righteous man standing among them, as happened during the plague of the Egyptian firstborn, and similarly with other plagues; three people would sleep under one blanket, and two of them would die while the one in the middle was saved.

It seems, the fury went forth to kill the entire congregation, [for complaining to Moshe, saying, "You have killed G-d's people"] slaying them by the same death as [Korach and his party] in whose path they followed, either swallowing them in an opening of the earth or consuming them by fire. These are all-inclusive punishments which kill everyone standing there, unless a miracle saves certain individuals [standing in the group].

It could be that the Holy One, blessed be He, said [*Remove yourselves from among this assembly*] in honor of the righteous men, for as long as they were among them He would not stretch out His hand against them. The commands ["Remove yourselves;" "Separate yourselves"] and others like them let Moshe and Aharon know that B'nei Yisrael needed their prayers for mercy and forgiveness, and Moshe did so immediately.

THE PRIVILEGE OF PRIESTHOOD

18:7 **I have presented your priesthood as a service that is a gift . . .** [What is "a service that is a gift"?] Rashi explains: G-d is giving you [the priesthood] as an exclusive gift, and *any unauthorized person that participates shall die* [by Heavenly punishment].

It seems to me that the correct interpretation is: You must perform the service of the priesthood, but do not consider it like a mandatory assignment of a servant of the king, but rather *as a service that is a gift* through which you will attain glory and splendor from Me. The Gemara in *Sotah* 15a expounds: [The priestly gifts of portions of the offerings are given] "for distinction" (18:8) as a mark of eminence, [to be eaten by the kohanim] in the same way kings eat their food.

חקת

Chukas

———◆———

What was Moshe and Aharon's Error?

20:1-12 B'nei Yisrael, the whole assembly, arrived at the wilderness of Tzin . . . There was no water for the congregation and they gathered upon Moshe and Aharon. The nation quarreled with Moshe . . . Hashem spoke to Moshe saying, Take the staff and gather the congregation, you and your brother Aharon. You should speak to the rock before their eyes and it will give its waters . . . And Moshe took the staff from before Hashem as he was commanded. Moshe and Aharon then assembled the congregation before the rock, and he said to them . . . "Shall we produce water for you from this rock!" Moshe raised his hand and struck the rock twice with his staff, and an abundance of water came out of the rock. The congregation and their animals drank. Hashem said to Moshe and Aharon, "Because you did not have enough faith in Me to sanctify Me before the eyes of B'nei Yisrael, therefore you will not bring this nation to the land that I gave them.

The sin of Moshe and Aharon by *Mei Merivah* "Waters of Quarreling" is not spelled out in the Torah. Rashi explains (20:11,12) that [they sinned by striking the rock] instead of speaking to it as G-d had commanded (20:7). Had they spoken [to the rock], G-d's name would have been sanctified before the whole assembly when [it gave forth water. The people] would have said: "If this rock which can neither hear nor speak fulfills the command of the Holy One, blessed be He, surely we [should fulfill His commandments.]" [End of Rashi's commentary].

This Aggadic interpretation, does not clarify the matter sufficiently. G-d's command to Moshe, *Take the staff*, implied that he should strike [the rock] with it. Had G-d wanted him to speak [to the rock], why tell him to take the staff in his hand? By the plagues in Egypt G-d said, *Take in your hand the staff that was transformed into a snake* (*Shemos* 7:15) in order to strike with it. Sometimes He said, *Point your staff* (8:1, 9:22, 10:12), when He wanted Moshe to strike with the staff, since the Torah omits things that are self-understood. Moreover, speaking to the rock is not a greater miracle than striking the rock; for as far as a rock is concerned speaking and striking it are all the same.

Furthermore, why did G-d say, *This is because you broke faith with Me* (*Devarim* 32:51)? [It cannot be because they failed to speak to the rock], for indeed they fulfilled the command to speak to the rock as mentioned at the occurrence of the event! Moshe and Aharon were commanded to tell B'nei Yisrael in front of the rock that G-d would bring forth water from this rock. And [they] did exactly that, as it says, *Moshe and Aharon then assembled the congregation before the rock, and he said to them . . . "Shall we produce water for you from this rock!"* (20:10). Thus the rock did "hear" when Moshe said this to the people! [So, why did G-d say Moshe and Aharon broke faith?]

RAMBAN REFUTES IBN EZRA'S VIEW

The commentators offer various explanations for the nature of the sin, and Rabbi Avraham ibn Ezra disproved many of them.

But the secret[21] to which he alludes is not correct either. If Moshe's attachment to G-d was interrupted because of the quarrel with the people, and he could not speak to the rock, making it produce water at the first try, but did have the rock produce water when he struck it a second time, after his attachment to G-d was restored, then he sinned the first time [when his attachment to G-d was broken]. But this sin would not cause G-d to say, *Because you did not have enough faith in Me to sanctify Me before the eyes of B'nei Yisrael* (20:12), since there was no lack of faith here at all.

THE RAMBAM'S VIEW

Rabbi Moshe [ben Maimon, the Rambam] explains [at the end of chapter 4 of *Shemonah Perakim*] that Moshe sinned by deviating from moderation and patience] to the extreme of anger when he shouted, *"Listen now, you rebels!"* Hashem disapproved of a man of his stature showing unwarranted anger in front of all Yisrael. This behavior is a *chillul Hashem* (desecration of G-d's name), because people emulate him, imitating his conduct and words, in the hope of attaining happiness in this world and the World to Come. They could not imagine Moshe displaying anger, which is a harmful character trait stemming from an evil disposition of the soul. Thus Hashem's words, [castigating Moshe and Aharon,] *You rebelled against My word* (27:14) may be explained as follows: Moshe was not speaking to ignorant or unworthy people, but to an assembly, the least of whose women, was on the level of the prophet Yechezkel ben Buzi, as our Sages say. Whatever Moshe said or did was carefully examined by everyone, so when he became

---

21 Brief summary of ibn Ezra's commentary: A perfect man like Moshe, being attached to G-d, can change nature and perform miracles. When B'nei Yisrael angered Moshe, and he had to speak to them, his attachment to Hashem was interrupted, so he lost his power to perform miracles. Therefore, when he struck the rock it did not produce water. He then restored his attachment to G-d, and when he struck the rock a second time water came forth (*Mekor Chaim*).

enraged, they would say: "Moshe has no moral shortcoming; He would not be angry with us, unless he knew Hashem was angry with us for demanding water, so we must have aroused Hashem's fury." However, we do not find that Hashem was angry [with the people] when He spoke to Moshe about this matter. Rather He said, *Take the staff and assemble the community . . . and allow the community and their livestock to drink* (20:8).

Thus we explain one of the most puzzling passages in the Torah, about which many commentaries have been written. Compare the explanations of other commentators on this subject with what we have said, and let the truth show the way. End of the Rambam's remarks. [Thus, in the Rambam's view Moshe and Aharon sinned by causing B'nei Yisrael to think Hashem was angry with them, when, in fact, He was not.]

RAMBAN REFUTES RAMBAM'S INTERPRETATION

[The Rambam] has added futility to the futility [of the other commentators]. For [Hashem said to Moshe,] *You rebelled against My word* (27:14), meaning that [Moshe and Aharon] transgressed His command, and G-d further says, *Because you did not believe in Me* (20:12), meaning they lacked faith in Him; not that they became angry.

Secondly, [if Moshe was punished for showing anger,] surely he deserved to be punished when he was needlessly angry with the commanders of the army (31:14).

Moreover, the verse does not say he was angry, "*Listen now, you rebels!* (20:10) was said in a way of reprimand, as in, *You have been rebelling against Hashem* (*Devarim* 9:24).

Additionally, Aharon never became angry in his life. He always walked in peace and fairness, [yet Aharon was also punished (20:12)].

Furthermore, it is impossible to suggest G-d was not angry with B'nei Yisrael for quarreling with Moshe. [We know that] their greatest sin was saying, "Why did you bring us out of Egypt. We would have rather remained slaves to our enemies doing hard labor than be the nation of Hashem, like children serving their Father." And the Torah [compares their complaint, "Who will give us some meat to eat?", to wanting to return to Egypt, saying,] *This is because you rejected G-d now that He is among you, and you whined before Him, "Why did we ever leave Egypt?"* (11:20), [and the chapter ends, *Hashem's anger was displayed against the people, and Hashem struck them with an extremely severe plague* (11:33)]

The first time [they asked for water] they said even less than this, griping, *Why did you bring us out of Egypt? Do you want to make me, my children and my livestock die of thirst?*" (*Shemos* 17:3), yet G-d was angry, considering it a great sin, as it says, *[Moshe] named the place* Massah uMerivah *"Testing and Argument" because the people argued and tested Hashem* (17:7). Here too, it says explicitly, *These are the Waters of Dispute* (Mei Merivah) *where B'nei Yisrael disputed with Hashem* (20:13). Can there be a greater sin than quarreling with the Creator? [Yet the Rambam says G-d was not angry with B'nei Yisrael!]

And, Moshe said, *Hashem also displayed anger at me because of you, saying "You too will not enter [the land]"* (*Devarim* 1:37). So you see, B'nei Yisrael sinned, causing this misfortune. Yet according to the Rambam, they did not sin in this entire episode!

Regarding the Rambam's statement: "G-d was not angry with the people [when He spoke to Moshe about this matter] but merely said, *Take the staff . . .* (20:8),"—know that whenever B'nei Yisrael needed something for their sustenance, even if they complained and sinned [in asking for it], *He, the Merciful One, is forgiving of iniquity and does not destroy, and arouse His entire anger* (*Tehillim* 78:38). He gives them what they ask for, overlooking their sin. Similarly, the first time they asked for water (*Shemos* 17:2), He gently said to Moshe, *March in front of the people . . .* (17:5), even though it involved trial and quarreling, evoking a warning to future generation, [*Do not test Hashem, your G-d as you tested Him in Massah* (*Devarim* 6:16)].

So too, in connection with the manna, G-d said to B'nei Yisrael in a loving and affectionate way, *I will make bread rain down to you from the sky* (*Shemos* 16:4). Only at the end, when G-d spoke again, did He say, *I have heard the complaint of B'nei Yisrael* (16:12), just to let them know they had sinned. Only when they complained without good reason did He unleash His anger on them.

Indeed, it hints here that G-d was very angry with B'nei Yisrael, and they deserved to die in a plague, for it says, . . . *and G-d's glory appeared to them* (17:6). "To them" refers to the congregation, [not Moshe and Aharon]. And this is the "vision of G-d's glory" that is manifest in [other] plagues, as was the case with the spies (17:10), and on the day of Korach's calamity (16:19) and on the day after (17:7).

There is one more reason to challenge the Rambam's view [that Hashem was not angry with B'nei Yisrael]. The verse expressly says, *They provoked anger at the "Waters of Strife," and Moshe suffered because of them* (*Tehillim* 106:32).[22] The passage counts this sin as one of the great trials with which B'nei Yisrael tested G-d in the wilderness.

RABBEINU CHANANEL'S VIEW

Rabbeinu Chananel's explanation is the most convincing and will suffice to answer one who questions the sin. He says they sinned by asking the rhetorical question, *"Shall we produce water for you from this rock?"* (20:10), but they should have said, "Shall *Hashem* produce water for you?" just as they said, *"In the evening, Hashem will give you meat to eat"* (*Shemos* 16:8). Whenever they announced a miracle, Moshe and Aharon said it was Hashem who performs the wonders for them; [since they did not say this here] perhaps the people thought Moshe and Aharon produced water with their own ingenuity. This explains why [G-d reproached them,

---

22 Perhaps the Rambam interprets the verse as, "They provoked Moshe's anger at the Waters of Strife."

saying,] *Because you did not sanctify Me among B'nei Yisrael* (*Devarim* 32:51) [by failing to tell them I am the One who performed the miracle].

At the previous incident [when water came forth] from the rock at Chorev, G-d said, *I will stand before you there on the rock at Chorev along with the elders of Yisrael* (*Shemos* 17:6). The seventy elders saw the pillar of the cloud hovering over the rock, thus the miracle became known to everyone, and they understood it was an act of the Great G-d. But here the people did not see anything, and they misunderstood the words of Moshe and Aharon [thinking that they themselves brought forth water from the rock].

It is possible that G-d said, *This is because you broke faith with Me* [using the words *me'altem bi*] (*Devarim* 32:51), because one who derives benefit from a sacred object is called *mo'el* [and Moshe and Aharon derived benefit from the miracle, because their esteem rose when the people thought they had produced the water]. Similarly, G-d said [to Moshe and Aharon,] *Because you rebelled [*merisem*] against My commandment* (*Bamidbar* 27:14), for G-d commanded, *Speak to the rock before their eyes* (20:8), [and the intent of "before their eyes" is] in order that I become sanctified in their eyes. It could be the meaning of *merisem pi* is: "you have changed My commandment," as in, *Vatemer es mishpatai*, "She changed My laws" (*Yechezkel* 5:6),[23] since I did not command you to use the phrase ["Shall *we* produce water for you" (20:10)].

According to Rabbeinu Chananel's explanation, in the phrase *Because you did not believe [*he'emantem*] in Me* (20:12), *he'emantem* is a transitive verb referring to B'nei Yisrael [not to Moshe and Aharon but meaning: you did not cause B'nei Yisrael to believe in Me, because you did not attribute the miracle to Me]. Or [if you say *he'emantem* is not a transitive verb,] it means "strengthening," as in the verses, *a strict order* [amanah] *for the singers* (*Nechemiah* 11:23), and, *the peg is affixed in a* [ne'eman] *secure place* (*Yeshayah* 22:25). In that case the verse means: "Because you did not

---

23 *merisem* is seen as related to *vatemer.*

strengthen yourselves to sanctify Me in their eyes."

However the truth is that this sin is one of the great mystical secrets of the Torah . . .

THE COPPER SNAKE

21:6,9 **And Hashem sent against the nation fiery serpents and they bit the people. A great multitude of Yisrael died. Hashem said to Moshe, make a serpent and place it on a pole, and anyone who was bitten, will look at it and live. Moshe made a copper snake** . . . Rashi explains: He was not told to make it of copper, but Moshe said: The Holy One, blessed be He, told me to make a *nachash*, "snake." I will make it out of *nechoshes*, "copper,"—as a play on words. End of Rashi's commentary, based on the words of the Rabbis.

I do not understand this, because G-d did not mention the word *nachash*, rather He told him to make a *saraf* "a fiery serpent" (21:8). The Rabbis [of the *Midrash*] meant that Moshe made it of copper to match the word *nachash* since this is the name of the species.

A MIRACLE WITHIN A MIRACLE

It seems to me [G-d told Moshe to make a fiery serpent] because all the deeds of the Torah are a miracle within a miracle. Thus the Torah removes an injury by applying the cause of the injury; it heals disease by means of the disease. Thus the Rabbis [in *Mechilta*] said in connection with the verse, *Hashem showed [Moshe] a certain tree* (*Shemos* 15:25), [the tree was bitter like the water, yet when he threw it into the water it made the water sweet], and Elisha cured the [brackish] water by throwing salt into it (2 *Melachim* 2:21).

It is a well-known medical rule that people bitten by poisonous animals become dangerously ill when they see [the animal], or its image; so that people bitten by a rabid dog or animal, if they look into water and see the image of the dog or animal that bit them, they will die, as is written in medical books and in the Gemara in *Yoma* 84a. Doctors are careful to avoid mentioning the name of the animal that bit him in the victim's presence. With the mentioning of [the animal], the victim's mind becomes obsessed with thoughts [of the bite] and he cannot cast it off until it causes his death.

A Scientific Experiment

The doctors mention a tried and tested experiment—one of the wonders of nature—regarding a person who became insane from a bite of a rabid dog. [They found] the image of small dogs, in his urine when it was placed in a glass cup. When the urine was passed through a strainer the image disappeared, yet when it was put back into the glass cup, the image of the little dogs was clearly seen after a short while. This true fact, is one of the marvels of the powers of the soul.

In light of this evidence, one would expect people bitten by fiery snakes to avoid looking at, mentioning, or even thinking about snakes. Despite this, the Holy One, blessed be He, commanded Moshe to make an image of the fiery serpent that killed them. Fiery serpents have red eyes, broad heads, and their necks are the color of copper. The only way Moshe could fulfill the command to make a fiery serpent was to make a copper snake, because it looks like a fiery serpent. Had he made it of any other material, it would look like a snake but not like a fiery serpent.

The Rabbis [quoted by Rashi] who said Moshe made the snake of copper as a play on words [*nechash nechoshes*] meant that the mere thought of the word *nachash* would be fatal [to one who was bitten by a snake, and he made it of *nechoshes* which sounds like *nachash* in order to magnify the miracle of their cure.]

To summarize: G-d commanded that they should be healed by

means of a poisonous substance, which would normally be lethal. Therefore Moshe made the *nachash* (snake) of *nechoshes* (copper) which sounds like *nachash*. And G-d said when a person who was bitten gazes intently at the copper serpent which resembles the deadly snake, he will live, so they will know it is G-d who sends death and gives life.

בלק
BALAK

⇒◉⇐

AN AMBIVALENT PERMISSION

[**B**alak, king of Moav, sent messengers to Bilam to hire him to curse B'nei Yisrael. G-d told him "Do not go with them and do not curse the nation for they are blessed". Balak again sent agents to Bilam and he told them he would ask G-d. G-d said "If the men come to summon you, get up and go with them, but you must do only as I tell you".]

22:20 **If the men have come to summon you . . .** At the beginning G-d told Bilam not to curse B'nei Yisrael for they are blessed; so why should he go [with Balak's emissaries] if he could not curse them, since that was the only reason why they wanted him to come? Therefore [originally] G-d said, "Do not go with [the emissaries, so you will not be swayed by them] to curse Yisrael, because it is a blessed nation." It is self-understood that Bilam informed the emissaries of what G-d said [although the Torah does not mention it].

Balak sent another delegation because he did not believe [G-d had told Bilam this; he assumed Bilam was stalling in order to get a greater reward]. Therefore, he showed him greater honor by sending higher-ranking dignitaries, promising to increase his reward. Bilam replied that it was not a question of money or willingness. It depended on G-d's will, and he would consult G-d a second time. In this he acted properly, for what could he know of the Almighty's will. It is always good to listen to G-d's advice, for He guides sinners on the way, and He would let him know what to answer the delegates, or reveal to him what would happen to [the Moabites] in the future.

G-d answered: "I already told you the nation is blessed, and you cannot curse them. [You conveyed this to them,] yet they came back to you! The phrase, *If the men have come to summon you,* means: If they agree that you will not curse the nation, then, "*set out and go with them. But only do exactly as I instruct you*" (22:20). If I tell you to bless them, bless them without fear of Balak. Initially it was G-d's wish that he go with them, after telling them he would not curse Yisrael, but would conduct himself exactly as G-d commanded him. It was G-d's will that B'nei Yisrael be blessed by a prophet of the non-Jewish nations.[24]

Thus Bilam should have told Balak's dignitaries: "G-d gave me permission to go with you, because you invited me, on condition that I do not curse the people, and if He commands me to bless them, I bless them." Had he told them this, they would not have agreed, and would have turned their backs on him, for even on this second occasion Balak said: "*Please come and curse this nation for me*" (22:17), [indicating] that he did not want Bilam to come to predict the future, but only to curse the people.

But Bilam, driven by his desire to go with them, did not say anything to the delegation. Instead, he got up in the morning and saddling his female donkey, went with them, letting them think that he was willing to fulfill their wish. That is why, *G-d's anger flared because he was going* (22:22), for had he told them [what G-d said], he would not have gone with them [since they would not have agreed to his conditions.] Thus he desecrated G-d name, for by going with them without setting conditions, he let them think he

---

[24]   If a Jewish prophet would give blessings and foretell wonderful tidings, it would not be as great an honor for us as when a Jew-hating prophet of the nations is forced against his will to declare our praises. (*Rabbeinu Bachya* to 23:9).

was going with G-d's consent. They thought G-d gave him permission to curse the people, changing His mind about His earlier condition of, *Do not curse the people, for it is blessed* (22:12). Later, when he did not curse them, they would say G-d had gone back on His word once again, or that He was mocking them [by giving Bilam permission to curse Yisrael]. It would be sacrilege to ascribe this to Him. *The Eternal One of Yisrael does not lie and does not reconsider* (1 *Shemuel* 15:29).

Can a Donkey See an Angel?

22:23 The donkey saw Hashem's angel . . . G-d's angels are "individual thinking beings" which cannot be seen by the human eye. They have no physicality which can be perceived by sight. When they appear to a prophet or a man with *ruach hakodesh* (divine inspiration) such as Daniel had, they are seen through the "eye of the soul" when it attains the level of prophecy or the level below it.[25] But it is impossible for an animal to see an angel.

Therefore, the passage, *The she-donkey saw Hashem's angel*, means it sensed something that frightened it, making it stop in its tracks. It sensed an angel that came to prevent it from moving ahead. The word "saw" is similar to the verse *My heart saw much wisdom and knowledge* (*Koheles* 1:16), where "saw" means, "perceived," not see with the eye."

When this miracle happened to the she-donkey, and the Creator granted it the power of speech, it said to Bilam [admonishing him for striking it]: "*Have I been in the habit of doing this to you?*" (22:30), implying that it did not know why it did such a thing now, but was compelled to do so. Therefore it did not say: "Look, an angel of G-d is standing in front of me holding a drawn sword in his hand," because it had not reached this level of comprehension.

---

25 Daniel was not a prophet; his visions were of a stage below prophecy (*Megillah* 3a).

The verse, *The she-donkey saw an angel of Hashem with a drawn sword in his hand* (22:23), does not mean it actually saw the sword, much less the angel; it means since the angel was ready to strike, [the she-donkey] had a violent fit of trembling because it felt as if people were coming to slaughter it.

[Even] if we [were to] say that there are angels which appear in human form as we explained in Parshas Vayeira, and we were to say that they can be seen even by animals, why didn't Bilam see the angel, and why wasn't he stricken with blindness?

An Extraordinary Miracle

Possibly, just as G-d granted the donkey power of speech, He increased its power of vision, so that like a man, it could see [a spiritual being]. Why doesn't the Torah say, "Hashem uncovered the eyes of the she-donkey, and it saw the angel of Hashem," as it later says about Bilam, *Hashem uncovered Bilam's eyes, and he saw the angel of Hashem* (22:31)? Because for the donkey to [see the angel and speak] was a great miracle not just an uncovering of eyes". In fact, it was one of the ten things created on the first Shabbos eve, at twilight[26]. However, our Rabbis only mention the opening of the donkey's mouth, [and not its heightened power of vision in the Mishnah in *Avos*].

The miracle [of the donkey speaking] was to show Bilam that it is G-d *who gives man a mouth* [i.e., the power of speech] *or makes one dumb* (*Shemos* 4:11), to make him realize that since G-d has the power to open the mouth of the dumb, He surely has the power to silence those who can speak; if He wishes He can put the words He wants into the mouths of the dumb, for everything is in His power. It was also a warning to Bilam, a famous diviner and sorcerer, not to engage in witchcraft and curse Yisrael by means of sorcery.

---

26 *Avos* 5:9.

BILAM THE SORCERER

22:31 **Hashem uncovered Bilam's eyes** . . . From here we learn Bilam was not a prophet, for if he was, his eye would not have to be uncovered to see an angel. The phrase "uncovered his eyes" is used for someone who has not reached the level of prophecy, such as Elisha's young man (2 *Melachim* 6:17) and Hagar the Egyptian (*Bereishis* 21:19). It is not used in connection with prophets. Indeed, Bilam is characterized as *Bilam ben Beor the sorcerer* (*Yehoshua* 13:22).

Although Bilam said, *as Hashem will speak to me* (22:8) [seeming to indicate that he was a prophet, he meant that] when he predicted future events through sorcery, it was "the word of G-d". G-d only appeared to him that night [as He would to a prophet] in honor of Yisrael.

Afterwards he was granted "uncovering of his eyes" so he could see and speak to the angel. Finally, he attained the level of *"seeing the vision of Sha-dai"* (24:4); all this in honor of Yisrael.

When he returned to his land he reverted to his permanent status of sorcerer. Indeed the verse describing his death says, *B'nei Yisrael put Bilam ben Beor, the sorcerer, to the sword* (*Yehoshua* 13:22). G-d forbid, B'nei Yisrael would never harm a prophet of G-d! So the Midrash says: Bilam had a connection with *Ruach Hakodesh* (divine inspiration), but when he allied with Balak, the *Ruach Hakodesh* left him, and he resumed his status as sorcerer. Therefore he moaned: "I was an exalted [prophet], but Balak brought me down."

BLACK MAGIC DOES NOT AFFECT YISRAEL

23:23 **No black magic can [be effective] against Yaakov** . . . Rashi explains: [Jews] do not need sorcerers and diviners [to know the future.] Whenever Yaakov and Yisrael need to be told how G-d is acting and what His decrees in heaven are, they are

told by their prophets, or the *Urim* and *Tumim*[27] rather than re-
sorting to sorcery and black magic. [End of Rashi's commentary].

It seems to me that Bilam was a sorcerer, and Balak sent him
magical devices and messengers telling him, *I know that whomever
you bless* with your black magic *is blessed, and whomever you curse*
with sorcery *is cursed* (22:6). Therefore, Bilam answered: "No
black magic can harm or do good to Yaakov, neither can sorcery
hurt or benefit Yisrael, for at all times Yaakov and Yisrael are told
what G-d has wrought for them, for both evil and good happen to
them by Divine decree."

Bilam meant that [the Jews] are the portion of G-d. They are
not like other nations whose destiny is determined by guardian angels and stars; therefore, a sorcerer cannot harm them through
black magic and divination. Moshe expressed the same idea when
he said, *When you raise your eyes to the sky and see the sun, moon, stars
and other heavenly bodies . . . which Hashem your G-d has appor-
tioned for all the other nations under the heavens. But Hashem has
taken you . . . so that you would be His heritage nation* (*Devarim*
4:19,20), as I have explained in *parashas Acharei Mos* (*Vayikra*
18:25).

BILAM'S VISION OF THE AGE OF MASHIACH

24:14 **Come, I will advise you . . .** The present prophecy—
Bilam's fourth and last—refers to the age of Mashiach,
for Bilam's prophecies refer to a series of future events, each one
taking place later [than the preceding event]. In his first prophecy
(23:7-10) he said [at the present time] Yisrael is Hashem's portion
and His inheritance. In the second prophecy (23:18-24) he added

---

27   Moshe inserted into the fold of the Breastplate a slip of parchment containing
the Ineffable Name. It would cause the breastplate to light up. If read in the proper order, these letters presented complete and true answers to the questions the
Kohen Gadol would ask of G-d.

that at a later period they would conquer the Land, slaying its kings. In the third prophecy (24:3-9) he foresaw that [at a still later point in time] they would settle in the Land, multiply in it, appoint a king who would defeat Agag, and their kingdom would be further exalted, for he saw David being greatly glorified, as it says, *David realized that Hashem had established him as king over Yisrael, and that He had exalted his kingdom for the sake of His people Yisrael* (2 *Shemuel* 5:12).

In the present prophecy, his fourth and final one, Bilam looked into the distant future, seeing the era of Mashiach. Therefore, he said, *I see it, but not now, I perceive it, but not in the near future* (24:17), using an expression he did not use in his previous prophecies. He said that this is G-d's design which He plans to carry out in the end of days.

BILAM FORESEES AMALEK'S DESTRUCTION

24:20 **He saw Amalek and he said, "Amalek is the first among the nations, but in the end he will be destroyed".** Rashi explains: [Bilam] saw in prophecy the punishment of Amalek and said: *Amalek is the first among the nations.* [Amalek] was the first of all nations to attack Yisrael. Onkelos also translates it this way. *But in the end he will be destroyed* by Yisrael, for it says, *You must obliterate the memory of Amalek* (*Devarim* 25:19). End of Rashi's commentary.

Possibly the words "he saw" are meant literally, [He actually saw Amalek, not as Rashi explains, "he saw in prophecy"]. Since he was standing on the peak of Pe'or that overlooks the wasteland (23:28), he could see the territory of Amalek who lived on those heights. He said, Amalek is now the first among the nations, meaning Amalek is the leading nation, because they are strong and seasoned warriors. Otherwise, they would not have attacked Yisrael, and Moshe would not have had to choose [fighting] men, pray and—in spite of his weariness—hold up his hands [toward heaven]

(*Shemos* 17:9-11). He built an altar naming it "Hashem-is-my Miracle" (17:15), because he considered the defeat of Amalek a great miracle. Therefore [Bilam] said Amalek will be first among nations, but will end up in greater destruction than all the others, as G-d said, *I will totally obliterate the memory of Amalek from under the heaven* (17:14). Similarly, *the first oils* (*Amos* 6:6) means "choicest oils," which are counted first in quality. Also "first" means "the best" in, *the first of that which was to be destroyed* (1 *Shemuel* 15:21); and, *as "head" and chief over them* (*Shofetim* 11:11); and, *the "chief" spices* (*Shemos* 30:23).

DESTRUCTION OF THE ROMAN EMPIRE

24:24 **Warships shall come from the ports of the Kittim and will afflict Ashur and Eiver—but it too shall be destroyed forever.** *The Kittim* refers to the Romans, who will lay waste to Ashur (Assyria) who is mentioned later in this verse, *and Eiver* which means Yisrael. Thus Bilam says that [the Romans] will oppress both the captor [i.e., Ashur (Assyria)] and their captives [the Jews]. *But in the end they too*, the people of Kittim [i.e., the Romans] *shall be destroyed forever. . .*

THE FOURTH KINGDOM

[In a prophetic vision Daniel saw four beasts representing the four mighty kingdoms of the world, Babylonia, Persia, Greece and Rome.] Rabbi Avraham ibn Ezra says the fourth beast in Daniel's prophecy represents the Arab empire. But he is mistaken in including the Arab empire in the "four kingdoms." Terrified by the Arabs, he claimed that it was impossible that the great and mighty [Arab] empire not be counted among [the great powers of the world which Daniel saw in his vision].

This statement stems from a lack of knowledge, because the four kingdoms in Daniel's vision came to power one after the other, each one conquering the empire before it, capturing dominion [of the world] from it, and continuing the oppression and exile of the Jews during its reign. Therefore in his dream Daniel saw that the Kasdim [i.e., Chaldeans/Babylonians] would enslave us first, then the Persians would rise to power and enslave us, to be followed by the Greek empire, and finally the Romans would defeat [the Greeks] and seize power, oppressing the Jews until the end of the *galus*, for their kingdom will end only with the coming of Mashiach.

ROME IS THE "FOURTH KINGDOM"

Thus our *galus* will last until the end of the "four kingdoms" [Babylonia, Persia, Greece, and Rome]. Even if other empires will arise in the world during the reign of these four kingdoms, the verse does not mention them, nor did Daniel see them, for he did not need to see them in order to know when the *geulah* (the final redemption) will take place.

In the days of the Persian and Greek empires, and in our time, there are great empires in the world, besides those of Rome and Yishmael (Arabia), such as India, Romania, the Tatars, and others. If ibn Ezra was correct [in including the Arab empire as the "fourth kingdom,"] he should have included many more empires!

Furthermore it is common knowledge that Rome, and not the Arabs sent us into *galus* in the days of Vespasian and Titus. Therefore, no matter where we are, whether in Arab countries, India, or even Ethiopia, we are in the *galus* of Rome until Rome's memory is blotted out and we are redeemed from its regime. Who knows, perhaps the Arab empire will yet be destroyed before the coming of Mashiach!

The "fourth beast" is the one that sent us into *galus*, as it says *The horn waged war with the holy ones and prevailed over them* (*Daniel* 7:21). This means we will remain in this *galus* until the coming of Mashiach, as Daniel says, *Until the One of Ancient Days came and the holy supreme ones were granted justice, and the time came, and the holy ones inherited kingship* (*Daniel* 7:22).

Whoever understands Daniel's visions will find that this interpretation reflects the true meaning of the text. In his second vision Daniel saw the ram goring westward (8:4), symbolizing the Persian empire (8:20). The he-goat is the king of Greece (8:21), and the great horn (8:21) is Greece's first king Alexander who defeated Persia. It says, *At its mightiest the great horn was broken, and a semblance of four horns came up in its place* (8:8), referring to the four generals who succeeded Alexander after his death. The text continues, *Out of one of them emerged a little horn which grew greatly toward the south, toward the east toward the beautiful land* (8:9), and it says, *It exalted itself even up to the Master of the host; because of it the daily offering was suspended* (8:11).

This is clearly a reference to the Roman empire which came from Greece, since Kittim (Rome) was one of Yavan's (Greece) sons,[28] and it was the Romans who put a stop to the continual offering. Daniel saw both nations [Greece and Rome, in this vision] as one beast, the he-goat (6:21) one of whose four horns grew greatly and put a stop to the daily offering. There are other proofs like that [in *Daniel*], and the tradition of our Rabbis [that the fourth kingdom is the Roman empire] is true and needs no support.

---

[28] Bilam spoke about Kittim (24:24) which refers to Rome, and Kittim was one of Yavan's sons (*Bereishis* 104), Yavan being the ancestor of the Greek people.

מסעי

MAS'EI

———◆———

THE ENCAMPMENTS ALONG THE WAY

33:1 **These are the journeys of B'nei Yisrael.** After taking revenge against Midian when G-d told Moshe, *Then you [shall die and] be gathered to your people* (31:1), and after allocating the land of Sichon and Og [to the tribes of Reuven, Gad, and half the tribe of Menasheh], where they built the cities mentioned above (32:34-38), Moshe wrote down the journeys; [knowing that this was his last opportunity]. This displayed G-d's kindness, because notwithstanding the decree to wander in the wilderness forty years, they did not constantly wander from place to place without rest, rather during this long period of time there were only forty-two encampments, as Rashi says, quoting Rabbi Moshe Hadarshan.

WHY ALL THE JOURNEYS WERE RECORDED

In *Moreh Nevuchim*, the Rambam 3:50 adds an additional benefit to be derived from knowing the names of all the stations along the way. He writes: "It was essential that the stops on their journeys be recorded, for miracles are convincing only to those who witness them; it is possible that later generations, knowing them only from hearsay, may deny that they happened. One of the greatest miracles in the Torah is the stay of B'nei Yisrael in the wilderness for forty years with a daily supply of manna. The places they traveled were remote from cultivated and inhabited land, and under normal circumstances one could not survive, for it is *not a place of seed, or fig, or grape, or pomegranate* (20:5). Indeed the Torah says, *You neither ate bread nor drank wine or strong drink* (*Devarim* 29:5). These miracles were witnessed by the people, but G-d knew that [in the future] people hearing about these miracles might doubt the veracity of these reports, just as they doubt the accuracy of other historical events. They might think the Jews stayed in the wilderness in a place not far from inhabited land, where it was possible for people to live [in the ordinary way], like the deserts where Arab Bedouins now live; or that they lived in places where they could plow, sow, and reap, or live on vegetables that grew there, and that there were water wells in those places. In order to remove these doubts, firmly establishing the authenticity of these miracles, the Torah enumerates the journeys, so future generations, seeing them, may learn about the greatness of the miracles which enabled humans to live in those places for forty years." The above are the words of the Rambam.

The recording of the [encampments on their] journeys was commanded by G-d, for it says, *Moshe recorded their stops . . . at G-d's command* (33:2) either for the reasons mentioned [by the Rambam] or for mystical reasons which have not been revealed to us. This differs from the opinion of Rabbi Avraham ibn Ezra who wrote that *at G-d's command* refers to *their journeys* [i.e. they made their journeys at G-d's command]. The Torah has already told this before, saying, *They remained camped at Hashem's word, and then moved on at G-d's word* (9:2).

ספר דברים
AN OVERVIEW

———◆———

MISHNEH TORAH—REVIEW OF THE TORAH

In this book, known as the "Review of the Torah," Moshe Rabbeinu speaking to the generation poised to enter the Land, explains most of the commandments affecting all Yisrael [i.e., non-kohanim]. He does not mention anything about priestly laws, offerings, ritual purity of the kohanim, or the duties [of the kohanim in the Beis Hamikdash], since he has already explained these matters to them. Being diligent by nature, kohanim do not need repeated warnings.

Moshe reiterates the commandments that apply to the *Yisraelim* [i.e., non-kohanim], either to clarify [the law], or to put the people on guard through repeated warnings. For example, he warns against idol worship, again and again, exhorting the people, and threatening them with terrifying punishments for committing sins.

LAWS NOT MENTIONED EARLIER

Moshe also adds in this book certain commandments not mentioned before, such as the mitzvah of *yibbum* (levirate marriage)[29] (*Devarim* 25:5,6), the law against maligning a married woman (22:13-19), the law of divorce and remarriage (24:1-3), the law of the conspiring witnesses (19:16-20), and others. These laws were all told to Moshe on Sinai or during the first year in the Tent of Meeting, before the episode of the spies. Nothing new was revealed to Moshe in the Plains of Moav [where he reviewed the Torah] except for the words of the covenant, as explicitly stated there (*Devarim* 29:69). [Since all the commandments mentioned in this book were given to Moshe before, either on Sinai or in the Tent of Meeting,] this book does not contain phrases such as, "Hashem spoke to Moshe, telling him to give B'nei Yisrael instructions," or, "Speak to B'nei Yisrael telling them this commandment."

Possibly these commandments were not written in the previous books when Moshe spoke to the people who left Egypt, since these commandments are observed only in Eretz Yisrael, even though they deal with personal conduct [which generally is not affected by land], such as the commandment of the wine libation [which is introduced with,] *When you come to your homeland* (*Bamidbar* 15:2)]. Or perhaps, since these commandments [such as *yibbum*, divorce, maligning] do not occur on a regular basis, Moshe only mentioned them to the generation which would inherit the Land.

ADMONITION AND ENCOURAGEMENT

Before Moshe explained the Torah, he admonished the people, reminding them of their many sins, and how they angered G-d in the wilderness, and yet, G-d treated them with compassion. Moshe wanted to make them realize G-d's kindness and to chasten them with his rebuke, so they would not backslide to their wrongdoing and be swept away because of their sins. [He also] wanted to

---

29   Under the law of *yibbum*, a childless man's brother has the obligation to marry his dead brother's wife.

encourage them with the knowledge that G-d always conducts Himself toward them with the attribute of Compassion; thus they will not think, "We will never inherit the Land, because no one is free from sin, and as soon as a person sins the attribute of Justice condemns him and destroys him." Therefore, Moshe stressed that the Holy One, blessed be He, the Merciful One, is full of compassion, for G-d's forgiveness and pardon, help a person to serve Him, as it says, *For with You is forgiveness, that You may be feared* (*Tehillim* 130:4). [If Hashem did not forgive sinners, they would stop fearing Him, saying: "We are despised by Him anyway, and will never find favor with Him, so what will we gain by serving Him!"]

ואתחנן
VA'ES'CHANAN

———◦《》◦———

TRANSMITTING THE REVELATION TO POSTERITY

4·9 **Only take heed and watch yourself very carefully so that
you do not forget the things your eyes saw . . .** Rashi
writes: Only, when you do not forget [the laws], performing them
in their authentic manner, will you be considered wise and under-
standing. But if you distort them because you forgot them, you will
be considered fools. End of Rashi's commentary.

This is incorrect.[30] In my opinion this verse is a negative commandment [i.e., prohibition], accompanied by a grave warning.
After Moshe told them, *they must keep all the commandments* (4:2),
and, *Safeguard and keep [these rules]* (4:6), he added: *"I am giving
you a strong-worded warning to take heed and watch yourselves very
much, to remember where these commandments originated, so you do
not forget the Revelation at Mount Sinai and all the things your eyes
saw there—the thunder and lightning, the glory and majesty of G-d,
and His words which you heard there out of the fire. And you should*

---

[30] According to Rashi, when Moshe said, *See! I have taught you rules and laws* (4:5)
he referred to the laws given at Sinai, and he follows this up with, *Only take heed . . .
so that you do not forget the things that your eyes saw . . . the day you stood at Chorev*
(4:9,10). But Ramban translates verse 4:5, *See, I teach you **today** rules and laws.*
Therefore, the phrase *so that you do not forget the things your eyes saw at Chorev*, cannot refer to *the rules and laws I teach you **today**.*

relate all the things you saw with your own eyes at this sublime revelation to your children and grandchildren forever." Moshe then explained that G-d gave this warning because He made this Revelation in order that we fear Him as long as we live, and teach this to our children for all generations to come. Therefore, do so, and do not forget it.

Before mentioning the Ten Commandments which were proclaimed on Mount Sinai, Moshe warned us with a negative commandment not to forget any detail of the Revelation, never letting it leave our hearts. He also commanded us through a positive commandment to pass on everything we saw and heard at Mount Sinai to all our children from generation to generation.

UNDENIABLE PROOF

This commandment has great benefit. If the words of the Torah reached us only through Moshe, when a prophet or a person having visions arises among us, presenting a sign or a miracle, and commanding us to do something that contravenes a commandment of the Torah, people may become doubtful, even though Moshe's prophecy was substantiated through miracles and wonders. But since our ears heard the Torah from the Almighty, and our eyes saw His glory, without an intermediary between Him and us, we can dismiss anyone disputing or casting doubt [on the words of the Torah], branding him a liar. No sign will help him, and no miracle will save him from the death penalty, for we know that he lied.

Therefore it says about the Revelation at Sinai, *They will then believe in you forever* (*Shemos* 19:9).[31] When we relate this to our children, they will know it is true beyond doubt, as if they themselves

---

[31] The Rambam writes: The revelation at Sinai is the only real proof that Moshe's prophecy was true and above suspicion . . . Before Sinai, the people did not believe with a faith that would last forever. [They might have believed, but] later would have doubts (*Yesodei Hatorah* 8:1)

had witnessed it. Knowing that we would not lie or impart point-less drivel to them, they will not have the slightest doubt about the testimony we give them. On the contrary, they will believe with certainty that we saw all this with our own eyes, and everything we tell them is true.

This theme will be discussed in *parashas Re'eih* in the section of the false prophet, beginning with the verse, *When there arises in your midst a prophet or a person who has visions* (13:2), and I already mentioned it in *parashas Yisro* (*Shemos* 19:9).

CREATION AND THE EXODUS

5:14,15 **And the seventh day shall be a day of rest to Hashem your G-d . . . in order that your servant and maidservant shall rest as you. And you should remember that you were a slave in the land of Egypt, and Hashem your G-d took you out from there with a strong hand and an out-stretched arm. It is for this reason that Hashem your G-d com-manded you to keep the Shabbos.**

Rabbi Avraham ibn Ezra writes: Because [He took you out of Egypt] He commanded you to [let your servants rest] on Shabbos. But this is not correct,[32] just as we say, "a remembrance of Creation" in the Friday night *Kiddush*, we also say "For that day is the first of the holy gatherings, a remembrance of the Exodus from Egypt." [Thus the Shabbos is given to remind us of the Exodus, not that the Exodus is the reason to let our servants rest.]

In *Moreh Nevuchim*, the Rambam explains (2:31) that The Ten Commandments in *parashas Yisro* tell us that the Shabbos is hon-ored and exalted. It says there, *Hashem therefore blessed the Shabbos and made it holy* (*Shemos* 20:11), explaining [that the Shabbos is exalted] *Because it was during the six weekdays that Hashem made the heaven . . . but on Shabbos He ceased working and was refreshed*

---

[32]   for it says, *to keep the Shabbos*, not "to do this on Shabbos."

(*Shemos* 31:17). In this parsha [*Va'es'chanan*] the Torah commands
us to observe the Shabbos [to remember] that we were slaves in
Egypt, forced against our will to work every day without rest. We
are commanded to abstain from work on Shabbos to remember the
kindnesses G-d bestowed on us by taking us from slavery to rest.

Thus, resting on Shabbos has a double purpose: (1) We affirm
our belief in Divine creation; that is, we believe the world was created, by G-d, and (2) We remember how kind G-d was in acquir-
ing us, making us His servants.

But this [explanation of the Rambam] does not seem reasonable
to me, for resting without doing any work on the seventh day does
not remind us of the Exodus; nor does anyone seeing us at leisure
conclude that G-d took us out of Egypt, one only sees us fulfilling
a commandment. However, Shabbos serves as a reminder of
Creation since we abstain from work on the day G-d *ceased working and was refreshed* (*Shemos* 31:17).

RAMBAN'S EXPLANATION

I think the following is a more suitable explanation: The Exodus
proves the existence of G-d, His power to create something out
of nothing, His acting with free will, and His omnipotence, as I explained in connection with the first of the Ten Commandments
(*Shemos* 20:2). This verse says: If you ever doubt that Shabbos
proves the world came into being [and thus had a beginning], and
that G-d is omnipotent and acts with freedom of will, then remember what your eyes saw at the Exodus. The Exodus proves
[He is the Master of the universe,] and reminds us [that He con-
trols nature and guides the events in the world].

Thus Shabbos reminds us of the Exodus and the Exodus reminds us of Shabbos, for on Shabbos we remember and declare
that G-d performs new signs and wonders in His creations, manip-
ulating them according to His will, since He brought everything
into being at Creation. The verse, *It is for this reason that Hashem*

your G-d has commanded you to keep the Shabbos [means: Through the awesome miracles you saw at the Exodus, you will understand G-d's command to keep the Shabbos.]

However, this verse [in *Ve'es'chanan*] does not reiterate that the reason for resting on Shabbos is, because *it was during the six week-days that Hashem made the heaven* . . . , because this was mentioned in the Torah many times. Instead, it says *The seventh day is Shabbos to Hashem* (5:14), meaning that on that day Hashem ceased working and was refreshed. The Torah adds that the Exodus also teaches us that He brought the world into being and ceased working.

PERMISSION TO SWEAR

6:13 **Remain in awe of Hashem your G-d, serve Him, and swear by His name** . . . The Rabbis opine, that the phrase, *and swear by His name*, means G-d gives us permission to swear by His Name. It is as if the Torah said: "Remain in awe of Hashem your G-d, nevertheless you may swear by His name, without being afraid." Since this permission was preceded by the commandment, *Remain in awe of Hashem and serve Him*, the Rabbis inferred that permission to swear is given only to one who has all the virtuous qualities [mentioned in 10:20, namely, fear of G-d, total devotion to Torah and mitzvos, and attachment to the *Shechinah*]. The meaning of the verse may also be: *Remain in awe of Hashem your G-d*, and His awe will weigh so heavily on you that His name will serve as an oath to you; when you want to confirm something, you will swear by His name. Even if you swore to your detriment, you will not violate your oath.

SERVE HASHEM BY GUARDING YOUR HEALTH

According to the Rabbis [in *Midrash Tanchuma*], *serve Him*, means considering yourself a servant bought by a master, serving his master at all times and placing his master's needs ahead of his own. Even his personal needs will be done as a service to G-d, in fulfillment of the dictum "All his deeds are done for the sake of Heaven" (*Avos* 2:17). He eats, sleeps, and takes care of his health in order to serve G-d, as the Midrash says: "The verse, *G-d saw all that He had made, and behold, it was very good* (*Bereishis* 1:31) refers to sleep. Is sleep good? Yes, because when you sleep a little, you rise [refreshed and ready] to engage in Torah study." Thus, when you take care of your bodily needs, have in mind, *I will praise Hashem while I live, I will sing praises to G-d while I exist* (*Tehillim* 146:2). This is a correct interpretation.

Do Not Test G-D—Have Faith

6:16 **Do not test Hashem your G-d as you tested Him in Massah.**

As you tested Him in Massah means: Do not say: "If Hashem is with us and performs miracles for us, [we will keep the commandments]" or, "If we worship G-d and are successful with everything well with us, and plenty of food, we will observe His Torah." For at Massah (*Shemos* 17:7) the people did say in effect: "If we see that G-d miraculously gives us water, we will follow Him into the wilderness; if not, we will leave Him."

This was considered a great sin, for after they had proof through signs and wonders that Moshe was a prophet of G-d, and the message [to follow him into the desert] was true, they should not have done anything to test him. Doing this is testing whether there is a limit to G-d's power not testing the prophet!

In this verse Moshe prohibited all generations to test the Torah or the prophets, for one can not worship G-d with doubt in his heart, or ask for a wonder, or put Him to the test. G-d does not perform miracles for everyone whenever they want, nor should one serve Him only on condition of a reward. Rather, a person who serves G-d and observes the Torah, should accept pain and adversity as righteous judgment, not say like a fool, *It is useless to serve G-d! What gain is there for us that we have kept His watch, and that we walked submissively before Hashem, Master of Legions?* (*Malachi* 3:14).

Therefore, the Torah says, *Be very careful to keep the commandments of Hashem your G-d, as well as His testimonies and His decrees that He commanded you* (6:17). [The commandments] testify to the miracles He performed for you in the past, such as [the mitzvos of] *Pesach, matzah,* and *sukkah* [which recall the Exodus]. Keep the decrees (*chukim*) even though you do not know their reasons, for you can be sure He will be good to you [and reward you] in the end. You do not need confirmation of [the truth] of the Torah and the commandments, because you already have proof that they were given by G-d.

This is true for any prophecy uttered by a prophet who, through signs and wonders was proved to be a true prophet. Do not question his words, whether he foretells reward or punishment, and do not harbor doubt about G-d's ability to fulfill [the prophecy]. Have faith in the Torah and you will endure; have faith in G-d's prophets and you will be successful!

[Moshe] promised that ultimately the Jews will have honor when they take possession of the Land and vanquish their enemies, for this was the one great benefit this generation needed most. Future generations do not need to test [the reward] for fulfilling the commandments. Let them just ask their fathers and grandfathers, who will tell them the Torah and commandments are true. And so he continues, *In the future, your child may ask you . . .* (6:20) to the end of the *parashah.*

The Ethical and Moral Lifestyle

6:18 Do what is fair and good in Hashem's eyes, so that He will be good to you . . .

The plain meaning of the verse is: Be careful to keep the commandments, testimonies, and decrees of G-d, having in mind that you are doing this because it is upright and good in Hashem's eyes. The phrase *so that He will be good to you* promises that when you do what is upright in His eyes He will be good to you, for He does good to good and upright people who do mitzvos for the sake of heaven.

A beautiful *Midrash* on this verse by our Rabbis says: *What is upright and good* means agreeing to a compromise [in litigation] and being generous to your opponent. The intent [of this *Midrash*] is as follows: Initially Moshe told us to keep the commandments, testimonies, and decrees that G-d commanded us. In the present verse he adds that one should try to do what is fair and good even [in dealings about which] there are no commandments, because G-d loves what is good and fair.

This covers many situations, for it is impossible to spell out all the alternatives in one's relations with neighbors and friends, nor all possible business dealings and social and political situations that may arise. Therefore, after mentioning many [laws of ethics], such as, *Do not go around as a gossiper* (*Vayikra* 19:16), *Do not take revenge nor bear a grudge* (19:18), *Do not stand still when your neighbor's life is in danger* (19:16), *Do not curse the deaf* (19:14) and, *Stand up before a white head* (19:33) and the like, Moshe states in general terms that one should do what is good and fair in all situations. This includes agreeing to a compromise and being lenient [with your opponent], or allowing a neighbor right of first refusal[33], as is mentioned in the Gemara (Bava Metzia 108a), or [choosing as *chazzan* a person who has] led an exemplary life and speaks with people in a considerate way, (Taanis 16a). [Conduct yourself in an ethical way] so people describe you as "wholesome and upright" in all aspects.

---

[33] A neighbor has the first right to buy a property adjoining his property before the owner offers it to someone else.

THE CHILD'S QUESTIONS

6:20-24 **In the future, your child may ask you, "What are the testimonies, decrees and laws . . .** He begins by asking: To what do the commandments called "*eidos*—testimonies" testify? They include the mitzvos of *matzah, sukkah, pesach, Shabbos, tefillin,* and *mezuzah* which are reminders of the miracles and bear witness to them. Then he will ask: "What [are the reasons for] the *chukim* (decrees)?" since their reasons are hidden; Then [he will ask,] regarding the mishpatim laws, "What are the reasons for the different punishments for violating] the laws? One who does work on Shabbos is stoned, one who has intercourse with a mother and her daughter is burned, and one who sows mixed seeds receives forty lashes! He is not referring to the [*mishpatim*] laws that regulate civic and social life, such as the laws of the ox [that gores], the hole in the ground [that is left uncovered], the custodians [of other people's property], and the other laws in the Torah, for they are obviously fair and good.

THE ANSWER TO THE CHILD'S QUESTIONS

Moshe commanded us to relate the whole story of the Exodus, when answering these questions. The purpose is [not only to bear witness to the Exodus] but to expound on it, as it says in the Ten Commandments, *I am Hashem your G-d who brought you out of Egypt* (*Shemos* 20:2), letting the inquiring child know Hashem is the Creator, who acts with a free will and is Omnipotent, as was demonstrated to us at the Exodus. Therefore it says, *Hashem directed great and terrible miracles against Pharaoh . . . before our very eyes* (6:21)—for by knowing and witnessing the signs and miracles, we became aware that Hashem, our G-d, is the Supreme Being in heaven above and on earth—there is none other. We became aware of this at the Exodus, as I explained in the first commandment (*Shemos* 20:2). Therefore, it is only right for us to give honor to His name, for He is our Creator, who bestowed great kindness on us, commanding us to keep these testimonies, decrees, and laws [about which the child inquired].

To be in awe of Him (6:24)—refers to the [mitzvos called *eidos*] testimonies which remind us of His miracles. *For our good*—refers to the [mitzvos called *chukim*,] decrees, for they are good, since, although their reasons have not been revealed, there is no decree that has undesirable consequences in any way. *So that we would survive, even as we are today*—through the *mishpatim* laws. By keeping all [three kinds of mitzvos] we will live because they are all good, with nothing damaging in them. On the contrary, they lead to a good life.

And we will receive charity before Hashem our G-d meaning we will receive a good reward for doing all these mitzvos. The reward is called charity, because a slave owned by his master is obligated to serve him, if the master pays him for his work it is considered charity.

HASHEM LOVES THE JEWISH PEOPLE

7:7 **Not because you are more numerous than all the nations did Hashem—*chashak*—attach Himself to you—*vayivchar bachem*—and chose you, for you are the smallest of nations.**

Chashak means He bound Himself to you with a strong bond, so He will never be separated from you. This is like the word, *vachashukeihem,* in the phrase, "their bands shall be made of silver" (*Shemos* 27:10). *Vayivchar bachem,* "He chose you," means you shall be His treasure and inheritance. The verb *bachar* always implies "being preferred to others."

Moshe explains that [G-d attached Himself to you and preferred you] *because of Hashem's love for you*, because He saw you as more worthy to be selected for love than all the other nations. He saw no need to explain why [Jews are more worthy of being loved by G-d than other nations], because one chooses as a friend someone who will [remain loyal and] bear any suffering his friend may bring on him. The Jewish people fit this model better than any other people. The Rabbis (Beitzah 25b) said: There are three that stand out for their boldness: Yisrael among the nations . . . because Yisrael stuck with G-d in all trials. [When forced to convert to Christianity, Jews cried out defiantly:] "Either let us live as Jews or nail us to the cross!"

Hashem attached Himself to you. Because your fathers reached such [lofty spiritual heights] He gave them an oath in order that no sin should cause Him to renounce His promise to them. Therefore, *He brought you out with a mighty hand* (7:8) [meaning although you were not worthy of it]. *Liberating you from the slave house* is an allusion that He struck [the Egyptians] instead of you, [for you deserved to be struck because of your wrongful conduct], as it says, *I gave Egypt as your ransom, and Kush and Seva in your place* (*Yeshayah* 43:3).

REWARD AND PUNISHMENT

7:9,10 You must realize that Hashem your G-d is the Supreme Being, a faithful G-d who keeps His covenant and kindness to those that love Him and keep his commandments, for a thousand generations. And repays in kind to those that hate Him to his face to destroy him. He will not delay to those who hate Him, to his face He will repay him.

This realization comes [from the events at the Exodus] as I explained (above 6:20). You must realize from this that He is *the faithful G-d*, whose word will not remain unfulfilled, and *who keeps in mind the covenant and kindness for a thousand generations when it comes to those who love Him and keep His commandments and who fear His name*, just as he kept the covenant He made with your fathers for you. You must also realize that *He pays back His enemies* for their wickedness *in their lifetime to destroy them*, just as He destroyed the Egyptians and did not delay [their punishment until after their death].

This principle [of reward and punishment] is always in force. Although a wicked man sometimes lives to a ripe old age doing wicked things [and is not punished during his lifetime], this is only because of G-d's attribute of "Keeper of Kindness" mentioned above. [The evildoer] surely did some good deed for which he deserves to be rewarded, [and he will receive his punishment in the World to Come]. Regarding reward and punishment G-d always repays good deeds with goodness and punishes wickedness with evil.

It is possible that "His enemies" [who are destroyed in their lifetime, as mentioned in this verse] refers to outright evildoers who deny His existence and have no merit at all. The *Midrash* (Koheles Rabbah 7:32) says: Rabbi Yashiyah said: Because of three things the Holy One, blessed be He, is slow to anger with the wicked in this world: they may repent, they have kept commandments for which G-d rewards them in this world, or perhaps they will have righteous descendants. Indeed we find that G-d was slow to anger with [the wicked] Achaz because [the righteous] Chizkiyah [was destined] to descend from him, and with [the wicked] Amon, because [the righteous] Yoshiah came from him; and the righteous Mordechai descended from [the sinful] Shim'i. [People in these three categories] are not considered "His enemies."

עקב
EIKEV

———◉———

THE LESSON OF THE MANNA

8.2 **Remember the entire path along which Hashem your G-d led you these forty years in the desert, He sent hardships to test you to know what is in your heart, to determine whether you would keep His commandments or not.** [How does remembering the wandering in the desert lead to keeping the commandments?—Moshe] said: [The wandering through the desert] shows you that doing mitzvos brings about perfect good, and that a righteous man is never forsaken and in need of food, for G-d sustained you in the wilderness through the great miracle [of the manna] because you obeyed His commandments.

I already explained, *He sent hardships to test you to determine what is your heart, whether you would keep His commandments or not* in the chapter of the manna *(Shemos 16)*. [The manna] was a great test, because they did not know [how to survive] in the desert without a supply of food. They could not store the manna, since [only] one day's ration came down each day, and when the sun became hot it melted, and they were very hungry for it. In spite of this, they accepted [the hardship] in order to keep G-d's commandments, [agreeing] to go wherever G-d led them. G-d could have led them through the cities in the area, but He gave them this

74

trial [of subsisting on a day-to-day ration of food], to prove that
they would keep His commandments forever.

Admonition Against Self-Confidence

8:18 **You must remember that it is Hashem your G-d who
gives you the power to become prosperous.** Jews are
formidable warriors whom Yaakov and Moshe compared to lions
and wolves (Bereishis 49:9,27), and they defeated the Canaanite
kings in battle. Therefore Moshe said: "If you think *it was my own
strength and vigor that brought me all this success* (8:17), remember
Hashem took you out of Egypt, when you had no strength and
vigor at all. Also remember that He took care of your needs in the
barren wilderness. Know therefore, that it was G-d who enabled
you to achieve this victory which you may think you won with your
prowess." [Continuing with verse 19 and 20, Moshe says:] "But if
you forget G-d, your strength will wane, and you will be destroyed,
just like the nations that G-d is destroying before you. For those
who forsake G-d will perish."

G-d Defeats the Enemies

Moshe brings another proof that it was not their strength and
vigor that brought them success, saying: "Listen, Yisrael! I
am telling you the truth! You know these nations are greater and
more powerful than you. How can you defeat them in battle? They
have great cities, fortified to the skies. How can you possibly conquer them? They are also a great nation, as tall as giants, as you
have heard from the spies who saw them, and about whom you
have heard the old saying: "Who can stand up against them?"

When you recognize this, you will understand even today that
you will not be able to cross [the Yarden] into their territory unless you firmly believe that G-d shall cross [the Yarden] before you.

He is like a consuming fire, annihilating and subjugating [these na-
tions] before you. It is not the strength and power He gave you
that did this to these mighty [nations]; it is the hand of G-d that
did it. This is an allusion to what happened [during the conquest],
Hashem cast on them large stones from heaven (*Yehoshua* 10:11),
and, *There was no day before it or after it . . . for Hashem did battle
for Yisrael* (10:14). The fortified cities Moshe refers to (in verse
9:1) are an allusion to the walls of Yericho that fell before the Ark.

This thought was expressed by David, saying, *For not by their
sword did they possess the land, nor did their own arm help them; but
by Your right hand and the light of Your countenance—for You favored them* (*Tehillim* 44:4). The right hand of G-d and His arm
fought against their mighty ones, and the light of His countenance
which favored [Yisrael] gave them the strength to slay [the warriors
of the enemy] in battle.

In the same vein, it says, *Yet I destroyed the Amorite before
them—the Amorite—whose height was like the height of cedar trees
and who was mighty as oaks—and I destroyed his fruit above and his
roots below* (*Amos* 2:9). [The prophet Amos] focused on the
Amorites because they were the mightiest [of the Canaanite na-
tions], and it was G-d who destroyed them.

WARNING AGAINST SELF-RIGHTEOUSNESS

9:4 **Do not say to yourselves, "It was because of my virtue
that Hashem brought me to occupy this land."**

First [Moshe] warned the Jews against thinking their own
strength and valor made them victorious over the Canaanite kings,
pointing out that G-d gives them the power to win, and G-d
Himself conquered the mighty Canaanites and their fortified cities
through overt miracles. He then admonishes them against thinking
G-d did this because of their righteousness, stressing that G-d did
this only because of the wickedness of these nations.

This explains why these nations will be destroyed, but it does not justify why *Yisrael* was chosen to take over their land. Therefore, Moshe clarifies: It is not because of your virtue, your righteousness, and your basic integrity [that you will occupy the Land], but because of the wickedness of these nations they will be destroyed, and because of the oath He made to your fathers, you will take possession of the land, for your sin cannot cancel the gift He promised your fathers, since He gave it to them with an oath.

You may ask: Did Moshe not say: *Because of Hashem's love for you* (7:8), which is a clear indication that [the Jews are worthy] of G-d's love? For G-d only loves good people, because, *He despises the wicked and the lover of violence (Tehillim* 11:5). If so, why should they not possess the Land for their own righteousness. However [when he speaks of His love of Yisrael 7:8] He is speaking of Yisrael in its totality [throughout history], but in this verse (9:4) he is specifically admonishing the people standing in front of him, who had rebelled against G-d from the day they were in the wilderness.

THE EXCELLENCE OF ERETZ YISRAEL

11:10 **The land that you are about to occupy is not like Egypt which you have left, where you plant seeds and then water by foot like a vegetable garden . . .**

In its plain sense this verse is one of several warnings [Moshe gives in this chapter]. He says, *Safeguard the entire mandate . . . so that you will come to occupy the land . . . a land flowing with milk and honey* (11:8,9), for when G-d gives rain in its season, the land will produce its crops. However, bear in mind that this land is not like Egypt which can be irrigated [by carrying water to the fields] on foot from pools and rivers like a vegetable garden. [Eretz Yisrael] is a land of mountains and valleys which can only be irrigated by the rain. It requires G-d's constant scrutiny, because it is a thirsty land, needing rain all year. If you violate G-d's will, and He does not shower the land with blessed rains, it will be a very bad

[year]; nothing can be planted and nothing can grow, not even grass in its mountains.

All this is reviewed in the next section (11:13-17), *If you are careful to pay heed to My commandments . . . I will grant the fall and spring rains in your land at the proper times* this will be ongoing. And if you will not pay heed, *He will lock up the skies so that there will not be any rain . . . You will rapidly vanish from the good land*, for you cannot live there without rain.

This section warns us with the laws of nature. Although everything is under G-d's control, and G-d can also easily destroy the people of Egypt by drying up their rivers and streams, the Land of Canaan can be destroyed very quickly if He does not provide rain. [Eretz Yisrael is] like a sick person who needs greater merit and more prayer to be healed than a well person who needs merely to remain healthy. Similarly, a poor man must pray more intently to become wealthy than a rich man must pray to keep his wealth, *But Hashem will enlighten the eyes of both* (*Mishlei* 29:13).

Observe the Mitzvos in Exile

11:17,18 . . . **And you will be destroyed quickly from the good land that Hashem gives to you. Place these words of Mine on your hearts and souls and tie them as a sign on your arms and they shall be as tefillin between your eyes.**

Rashi explains: Even after you go into exile, be conspicuous through [the performance of commandments. For example,] put on *tefillin* and make *mezuzos* so that these mitzvos should not be new to you when you return [to Eretz Yisrael]. Similarly it says, *Make road markers for yourself* (*Yirmeyah* 31:20). [As you go into exile, mark your route, for you will come back home. According to Rashi the verse tells us to keep the mitzvos in *galus*].

I have already written on this subject. Since these commandments [*tefillin*, Torah study, and *mezuzah*] are personal obligations, and are therefore binding in all places, not just in Eretz Yisrael, [why does the Medrash imply that they are only done so we remain familiar with them?] This Midrash contains a profound secret which I alluded to earlier.[34] Moshe repeated the commandments of *tefillin*, Torah study, and *mezuzah*, a second time to hint that we will be required to observe them after being exiled from Eretz Yisrael. From these [two mitzvos] we learn that all commandments which are personal obligations must be observed in all places; when we are outside Eretz Yisrael we are only exempt from commandments that relate to the land, such heave-offerings and tithes. This is how it is interpreted in Sifrei ad loc.

By placing the mitzvah of tefillin after these words "you will be banished," the Midrash means to say that [Moshe implied that you must observe *tefillin* and all other mitzvos which are personal obligations even after you are exiled].

---

[34] In *Vayikra* 18:25.

ראה
RE'EIH

THE SOUL REMAINS INTACT AFTER DEATH

14:1,2 **You are children of Hashem your G-d, do not mutilate yourselves and do not place a bald spot between your eyes because of a death. For you are a holy people to Hashem your God.** Rabbi Avraham ibn Ezra writes: Since you are children of G-d, and He loves you more than a father loves his child, do not mutilate yourselves [as an expression of anguish] over anything He does. Whatever He does is for your good, even if you do not understand it, just as little children do not understand their father's actions yet rely on him. *For you are a holy people*—You are not like the other nations, therefore do not do as they do. [End of ibn Ezra's commentary].

[The Ramban comments:] In my opinion the expression "a holy people" is an assurance that the soul remains intact before G-d after death. Since you are a holy people and G-d's treasure, and He does not destroy the soul [of a sinner after he died,], rather He designs plans so no one is banished from Him, it is wrong for you to mutilate yourselves or to make a bald patch for the dead, even if the deceased died at a young age.

The Torah does not forbid weeping for the dead because it is natural to cry over the loss of a loved one. People cry even when a loved one leaves on a journey, in life.

By extension [to the prohibition against self-mutilation for the dead] the Rabbis said (Moed Katan 27b) that one should not mourn excessively.

SENSITIVITY AND COMPASSION

14:21 Do not eat any carcass . . . since you are a holy nation to Hashem your G-d, do not cook a kid in the milk of its mother.

Since you are a holy nation to Hashem your G-d, refers to, *Do not cook a kid in its mother's milk* which is the end of the verse, because meat cooked in milk is not disgusting. [The mixture] is only forbidden because we must be holy in our eating habits. [However eating a carcass, mentioned in the beginning of the verse, is in fact disgusting and the Torah does not prohibit it only because we are holy.]

Or perhaps, the intent of the prohibition [against cooking a kid in its mother's milk] is that we become a holy people—not cruel and heartless, drawing milk from a mother in order to cook its kid in it. Any meat cooked in any milk is included in this prohibition, because every nursing animal is a "mother" and every suckling young is a "kid," and cooking them together, is an act of cruelty.

שׁוֹפְטִים
SHOFETIM

———◦◉◦———

OBEY THE DECISION OF THE COURT

17:11 **Do not stray to the right or to the left from the word that [the court] declares to you.**

Rashi explains: Even if [the court] tells you right is left, or left is right obey them. Rashi means even if it is as obvious to you as distinguishing between your right and left hand, that [the judges] are mistaken, you must do as they command you. Do not say; "How can I eat this forbidden fat!" or, "How can I put this innocent man to death!" Say instead: "The Lord who gave the commandments ordered me to perform all His commandments according to the instructions of those who stand before Him in the Beis Hamikdash. He gave me the Torah on condition that I fulfill it as they understand it, even if they are mistaken." This is what happened when, Rabban Gamliel, [the head of the Sanhedrin,] ordered Rabbi Yehoshua [to come before him with his staff and money on the day Rabbi Yehoshua calculated would be Yom Kippur] and Rabbi Yehoshua obeyed.

This commandment is crucial, because the Torah was given to us in written form, and there are differences of opinion about the statutes derived from it. [Without this law] disagreements would abound, and the [indivisible] Torah would be fragmented into many Torahs. Therefore, G-d ordained that we listen to the Great

Court that stands before G-d in the place that He will choose, obeying everything they tell us regarding interpretations of the Torah, whether they received the interpretation [as a tradition reaching back] to Moshe who heard it from G-d, or whether their decision was based on their own interpretation. G-d gave us the Torah contingent on their interpretation [of the text], even if [their ruling] seems as absurd as mistaking right for left.

Certainly we must accept their opinion and believe that when they say "right" it is indeed right, and when they say "left" it is indeed left. For the spirit of G-d rests on those who serve in His Sanctuary. *He will not forsake His devout ones; they will be eternally protected* (*Tehillim* 37:28) from error and stumbling.

The wording of *Sifrei* is: "Even if it seems to you that [what they judge as] right is left and [what they judge as] left is right, you must obey them."

THE BANE OF PRIDE

17:19,20 **And it [the Torah scroll] shall be with him [the king], and he should read from it all the days of his life so that he should learn to fear Hashem . . . So that [the king] will not begin to feel superior to his brethren . . .** In this verse the Torah hints at the prohibition against haughtiness and arrogance. Since the Torah forbids even a king to be haughty and arrogant, surely people who have no reason to be proud are forbidden to be conceited. Even a king, who deserves to be glorified and exalted, is commanded to be humble like all his brethren of lower station. Because pride is a despicable character trait, G-d detests it even in a king. Only G-d is to be glorified and exalted, only He is to be praised. Man may take pride only [in knowing G-d], as King Shlomoh said, *Every haughty heart is the abomination of Hashem* (*Mishlei* 16:5), and as it says, *For only with this may man glorify himself—contemplating and knowing Me* (*Yirmeyah* 9:23).

TOTAL COMMITMENT TO G-D

18:13 **You must remain totally faithful to Hashem your G-d.** This means we must direct our hearts to Him, believing that He alone does everything, He knows the truth about future events, and we should inquire about the future from Him alone, or from His prophets, or from His devout ones, that is, the *Urim* and *Tummim*.[35] We may not consult astrologers about the future, believing that their prediction will come true in any shape or form. Instead, if we hear one of their predictions, we should say, "Everything is in the hands of Heaven," for He is the G-d of the powers, the Supreme Being, the Omnipotent, who changes the disposition of stars and constellations at His will, *Who abrogates the omens of the stargazers and makes fools of the astrologers* (*Yeshayah* 44:25). Believe that whatever happens to you is a reflection of the extent of your closeness to G-d.

Therefore, after the prohibition against inquiring from diviners about the future and consulting the dead [about the fate] of the living, [Moshe] says, *You must remain* [tamim] *totally faithful to Hashem, your G-d* in all these matters and not be afraid of fortunetellers. Instead, consult His prophet, and do as he says. This is consistent with the translation of Onkelos: "You shall be totally faithful in your fear of Hashem your G-d," meaning you shall not be lacking in your fear of Him. *Tamim* "whole" denotes "one who is totally committed," as in, *seh samim*, "a flawless lamb" (*Shemos* 12:5), without a defect or any imperfection. This verse is considered a positive commandment. I have already mentioned this in connection with the verse, *Veh'yei samim*, *"Be perfect"* (*Bereishis* 17:1).

---

[35] A slip of parchment containing the Ineffable Name was inserted into the fold of the Breastplate. When the Kohen Gadol was asked questions of national import, the individual letters on the stones of the Breastplate would light up. If read in the proper order, these letters presented true answers to these questions.

The Plotting Witnesses

[The Torah in this section deals with false witnesses. What the false witnesses tried to do to the accused is done to them as punishment.]

19:19 **You must do the same to him as he plotted to do . . .** Our Rabbis (Makkos 5b) deduced *as he plotted*—but not as he did. On the basis of this, the Rabbis said: If the plotting witnesses killed [i.e., if the one against whom they testified was actually killed because of their testimony,] they are not killed. End of Rashi's commentary.

[Logic would dictate that they should surely be executed if the one against whom they testified was executed.] However [they are not killed] because the punishment of the "plotting witnesses" is a Divine decree. [If G-d allowed them to be refuted before they killed, it shows they lied. But if G-d only allowed them to be refuted after they killed, it shows clearly that they told the truth.]

After all, they are two witnesses against two. [And why should we believe the second pair of witnesses more than the first?] But if two witnesses testified that Reuven killed a man, and two other witnesses refute them, the Torah decrees that the refuted witnesses should be killed. It was in the merit of Reuven who was innocent that the plotting witnesses were refuted. Had he been guilty and liable to the death penalty, G-d would not have saved him from judgment, for it says, *I will not let a guilty person escape punishment* (*Shemos* 23:7).

But if Reuven was executed, it shows clearly that the testimony of the first witnesses was true, and that he was lawfully executed. Had Reuven been innocent, G-d would not have abandoned him in their hands, as it says, *Hashem will not forsake him to his hand, not let him be condemned when he is judged* (*Tehillim* 37:33). Furthermore, G-d would not allow righteous judges who stand before Him, to spill innocent blood, *For judgment belongs to G-d* (*Devarim* 1:17), and, *In the midst of judges He shall judge* (*Tehillim* 82:1).

All this shows the high stature of Jewish judges, and is an assurance that the Holy One, blessed be He, agrees with them, and is with them when they sit in judgment. This is the meaning of the verse, *The two men who have testimony to refute* [*the false witnesses*] *shall stand before Hashem* (19:17). When they come to the priests and the judges they are standing *before Hashem*. G-d leads [the judges] in the path of truth. I mentioned this already in *Parashas Mishpatim* (*Shemos* 21:6).

Preparing for War

20:1 **When you go to battle against your enemies and see horses, war chariots—a people more numerous than you—do not fear them, because Hashem your G-d who took you up from Egypt is with you.** This is a new commandment which [Moshe] announced, since they were about to go to war.

The verse, *Hashem your G-d is the One who is going with you. He will fight for you against your enemies, and He will deliver you* (20:4) is an admonition not to be fainthearted, not to be afraid of the enemy, and not to rely on one's own valor, thinking: "We are strong and courageous fighters." Instead, turn your hearts toward G-d and rely on His help, believing that *He does not desire the strength of the horse, and He does not favor the legs of man* (*Tehillim* 147:110). *Hashem favors those who fear Him, those who hope for His kindness* (*Tehillim* 147:10,11).

[Moshe] says, *[Hashem] will fight for you against your enemies,* implying that He will make them fall before you by the sword. *And He will deliver you,* indicates that everyone will remain unharmed in the war, with not a single man lost. [In the natural course of events] even when one defeats his enemy there are many casualties, however Yehoshua was alarmed when about thirty-six men fell in the battle [of Ai] (*Yehoshua* 7:7), for not even a hair should have been lost in a war commanded by G-d; and [a war against the seven Canaanite nations] is G-d's war.

If this is so, why did the officers announce: "[One who recently built a house, planted a vineyard or married should return from the battlefield] . . . *so that he will not die in the war*" (20:5)? As a servant of G-d, the Kohen [Anointed for Battle] exhorted them to fear G-d, promising that not a single man would be lost. But the officers, speaking in terms of the normal course [of warfare] said: ". . . *So that he will not die in war.*" For even in victory, it is normal to expect casualties during war.

Because a man's heart is focused on [a new] house, vineyard, and wife, and he will flee because of them, people in these three categories were told to go home.

EXEMPTIONS FROM MILITARY SERVICE

20:8 The lower officers shall then continue speaking to the people and say, "Is there any man among you who is afraid or faint-hearted . . ." [Why be afraid if the Kohen just said there would be no casualties?] According to Rabbi Yose HaGelili, [who explains that the fainthearted are people who sinned and are afraid their sins made them unworthy of G-d's help,] the righteous will place their trust in G-d after hearing the Kohen's assurance that He will help, and no one would fall in battle. The officers then address those who are afraid because of their sins. The Torah [freed those with new homes . . .] to provide [one with sins] an opportunity to attribute his return home to his house, his vineyard, or his wife, hiding the fact that his return is because of sins he committed. *So that he will not die in war* means [the sinner] imagines [he will die] and may run away [although all those who trust the Kohen's assurance will not fall in battle].

In Rabbi Akiva's view, "fainthearted" is meant literally. [Cowardly people should go home,] because whoever is still afraid after hearing the assurances of the priest lacks faith in G-d, and is not worthy of the miracle [of surviving the battle] . . .

Miracles as a Last Resort

20:9 **The leaders of the legions shall take command to lead the people.** [Why do they take command of the legions when G-d promised to defeat the enemy without any Jewish casualties?] The Torah gives orders to be carried out by the natural order of things, while G-d secretly performs miracles for those who fear Him. He only changes the course of nature, if there is no other way of rescuing [the Jews], or to make His name known to His enemies, as was the case at the Parting of the Red Sea and similar events.

Offering a Peaceful Settlement

20:10 **When you approach a city to wage war against it, you must propose a peaceful settlement.** Rashi comments: This verse [which commands us to make a peaceful settlement] speaks of a war which is not obligatory [as opposed to a war ordained by the Torah, such as the conquest of the Land of Canaan], as stated explicitly at the end of this section, *That is what you must do to the cities that are very far from you* (20:15). End of Rashi's commentary.

Rashi is quoting *Sifrei,* where it says: "The verse speaks of a nonobligatory war." [Although it seems that *Sifrei* means a peaceful settlement must be offered only in voluntary wars,] however a peace settlement must be offered even in an obligatory war; even the seven indigenous nations must be offered a peaceful settlement. The teaching of the Rabbis refers to the later section which distinguishes between two kinds of wars [thus, *when the enemy responds peacefully, the people shall pay tax to you and serve you,* (20:11) refers to a voluntary war, but in an obligatory war the enemy must accept the seven Noachide commandments.[36]] Indeed we find that Moshe

---

[36] Prohibition against manslaughter, stealing, immorality, blasphemy, idol worship, eating a limb torn from a live animal, the obligation to establish courts of law.

offered peace to Sichon, king of the Amorites, (*Devarim* 2:26) and surely he did not violate both the positive and negative commandments in this section: *You must wipe them out completely* (20:17), and, *You shall not allow any people to remain alive* (20:16).

However, if they reject your peace offer, declaring war, then, the Torah commands you to strike down the adult males of distant cities by sword, keeping alive the women and male children. But you must wipe out even the women and children in the cities of these people [i.e., the seven Canaanite nations].

The same was said by the Rabbis in *Devarim Rabbah* (5:13), in *Tanchuma* (here), and in *Yerushalmi* (*Shevi'is* 6:1): Rabbi Shemuel bar Nachmani said: Yehoshua fulfilled the laws of this chapter. What did he do? He sent a notice to each place he planned to conquer, stating: "Whoever wishes to make peace, let him come and make peace; whoever wishes to leave, let him leave, and whoever wants to fight, let him come and fight." The Girgashites left. He made peace with the Gibeonites. The thirty-one kings [of Canaan] decided to make war, and the Holy One, blessed be He, struck them down." [Thus Yehoshua offered peace even in an obligatory war.]

The verse says the same in reference to the seven [Canaanite] nations: *There was not a city that made peace with B'nei Yisrael except for the Chivite inhabitants of Giv'on; they took everything in battle. For it was from Hashem to harden their hearts toward battle against Yisrael in order to destroy them* (*Yehoshua* 11:19,20). Had they wanted to make peace, Yehoshua would have made peace with them.

The difference between an optional and obligatory war [arises not only if the enemy rejects the peace offer,] but also with regard to making the peace offer. When we fight with distant cities we must propose peace on condition that they become our subjects, serving us. But we must propose peace to the cities of the [seven] nations, on condition that they pay taxes and serve us, and agree not to worship idols [observing the seven Noachide commandments]. The Torah does not mention [idolatry] here because it forbade this already in, *Do not allow them to reside in your land, since they may then make you sin to Me* (*Shemos* 23:33).

THE GIV'ONIM'S DECEPTION

20:11 **If they respond to you in peace and open to you, all the inhabitants shall pay tax to you and serve you.**

The episode of the Giv'onim (Gibeonites) [who tricked Yehoshua into making peace and concluding a treaty with them][37] happened because they did not know that Jews must propose peace before going to war; they made their deception before Yehoshua's [offer of a peaceful settlement] had reached them. For this reason they said, *We were most fearful for our lives because of you* (*Yehoshua* 9:24).

Or perhaps [the Giv'onim staged the deception because], they did not accept Yehoshua's offer at first, and later, terrified [that their belated acceptance of the peace proposal would be rejected,] they disguised themselves as strangers [claiming to seek an alliance with *B'nei Yisrael*,] as it says, *When the inhabitants of Giv'on learned how Yehoshua had treated Yericho and Ai, they for their part resorted to cunning* (*Yehoshua* 9:3), [hoping to avoid being killed by the Jews.] They also wanted to become their allies, rather than their servants.

The Jews were angry, [and did not propose a peaceful settlement when they discovered the Giv'onim were Canaanites]. They would have killed them had it not been for the oath the leaders had given [not to harm them (9:19)]. The Giv'onim should have accepted to pay taxes and become servants, as we said. Instead, the Jewish leaders made a treaty with them, making them their equals and allies.

Yehoshua made peace with them because he thought they came from distant cities which B'nei Yisrael never intended to capture.[38] Therefore, Yehoshua cursed them, saying, *Now you are cursed* (9:23), implying: You are of the accursed nations that were cursed by G-d. He treated them according to the law that applies to them, namely, *They shall pay tax to you and serve you*, making them *woodchoppers and water drawers for the assembly and for the Altar of Hashem* (9:27). This constituted "tax and servitude," as we explained.

---

[37] *Yehoshua* 9:3-27.
[38] Only distant cities that were scheduled to be conquered had to submit to taxes and servitude; not so cities which were not on the agenda.

Some explain the verse, *If the city responds peacefully* (*Devarim* 20:11) to mean: If the city responds peacefully when the peace proposal is first made, but if they reject the offer, we do not accept a later peaceful response.

The Rambam writes that the leaders were angry with [the Giv'onim] for duping them into making a treaty with them, when it says, *Do not make a treaty with [these nations] or with their gods* (*Shemos* 23:32).

I do not think this is correct, because the Giv'onim surely agreed to give up idol worship, for they said, *Your servants have come for the sake of Hashem, your G-d* (*Yehoshua* 9:9). Therefore, Yehoshua did not have to warn them about serving G-d, and B'nei Yisrael were permitted to make a treaty with them, just as the Giv'onim were allowed to reside in the Land, for both [making the treaty, and letting them live in the Land] are forbidden only before [the inhabitants] repent [of their idol worship] as it says, *Do not make a treaty with [these nations] or with their gods. Do not allow them to reside in your land, since they then make you sin to Me* (*Shemos* 23:32,33). But the explanation of the Giv'onim episode is as I have said.

THE CALF WHOSE NECK WAS BROKEN

[This portion of the Torah deals with the situation where a corpse was found outside of a city. The closest city must bring a calf to a barren valley, breaking its neck there.]

21:4 **The elders of the city shall bring the calf to a harsh valley which has not been worked or sown, and they break its neck there in the valley.**

Rabbi Avraham ibn Ezra explains the breaking of the calf's neck as follows: G-d commanded that the city closest to the corpse bring this atonement, because a man would not have been murdered in their environs had they not done a similar sin. G-d's thoughts are exceedingly profound to us.

However the Rambam in *Moreh Nevuchim* (3:40) writes that the
purpose [of this ceremony] is to find the murderer, ridding themselves [of the guilt] of innocent blood, for in most cases the murderer comes from the city nearest the corpse. When the elders [of
the Great Sanhedrin] measure [which city is the closest to the
corpse], and the elders of that city testify before G-d that they were
not careless about keeping the roads in good condition and protecting them, and that they do not know who killed the man, and
then the elders bring the calf, people talk about it; by making the
event public, the murderer may be found out. Indeed, the Gemara
Yerushalmi in *Sotah* 9:1 says, Even if a maid says: "So-and-so is the
murderer" the calf is not killed. It is a grave crime if one knows who
the murderer is, yet does not reveal it, after hearing the elders testify before G-d that they do not know who he is. Anyone with even
the slightest bit of information that might lead to the arrest of the
killer will report it and the crime will be solved, with the murderer
being executed by the court, the king or the avenger. The land
where the calf's neck is broken may never be tilled or sown again,
drawing added attention to the case, since whoever sees the place
will recognize and talk about it.[39] End of the Rambam's comments.

[The Ramban comments:] According to [the Rambam's] line of
thinking, the ceremony holds an indirect benefit [since it may lead
to the capture of the killer], but the breaking of the calf's neck itself has no inherent purpose. If so, the ceremony should be in a fertile field, where people can notice it is not being tilled, rather than
in a "harsh valley" where people do not notice it is not tilled.

In my view the reason for the *eglah arufah* ceremony is the same
as that for sacrifices brought outside the Court of the Beis
Hamikdash, namely, the goat sent to Azazel and the Red Cow.
Therefore, the Rabbis counted the law of the *eglah arufah*—"the
calf whose neck was broken"—among the *chukim* [laws whose reasons are not known].

---

[39] The Rambam adds: The owner of the land will do all in his power to find the
murderer, in order that the calf should not be killed and his land should not become
useless to him.

KI SETZEI

———— ✦ ————

THE REASONS FOR THE MITZVOS

22:6 **If you come across a bird's nest . . . and the mother is sitting on her eggs or chicks, do not take the mother from upon her chicks.**

This commandment and the commandment of, *Do not slaughter [a female animal] and its child on the same day* (*Vayikra* 22:26), are instituted to instill compassion in our hearts. Perhaps the Torah does not permit us to destroy an entire species of animal, for although the slaughter of a single animal is permitted, if one kills a female animal and its young on the same day, or takes [birds] when they are free to fly, it is considered as if he wiped out that species.

According to the Rambam in *Moreh Nevuchim* (3:48) the reason for these commandments is to prevent people from killing the young in sight of its mother, since the pain of the animal under such circumstances is very great. There is no difference between the pain of man or other living beings, since the love and tenderness of a mother for her young ones is not produced by reasoning, but by imagination; a faculty which exists in most living beings. End of the Rambam's remarks.

According to the Rambam's reason, the prohibition against killing a mother and its young should apply only if one killed the young before its mother. However the Torah also prohibits killing

the mother before the young as a preventive measure so one won't
come to kill the young before the mother. It is more correct to say
the reason is to keep us from being heartless.

The Rambam adds: Do not challenge me by quoting the
Gemara (*Berachos* 33b) which says: "If one says in his prayer: 'Your
mercies extend even to a bird's nest,' he is silenced" [which seems
to indicate that having pity on the mother bird, is not the reason
for the commandment] for that Gemara follows the opinion of
Sages who hold that all commandments have no reason; they are
decrees of the Creator. But we follow the opinion [of the Sages]
who say the commandments have reasons.

The Rambam points to the following Midrash [which also seems
to contradict his notion that mitzvos have reasons]: What difference does it make to G-d whether an animal is slaughtered from
the throat or the back of the neck? The only reason for the mitzvos
is to refine and test the people [seeing whether they will keep G-d's
mitzvos,] as it says, *Every word of G-d is refined* (*Mishlei* 30:5)

PROOFS THAT MITZVOS HAVE REASONS

The Rambam's definitive conclusion that there is a reason for
the mitzvos is sound, because the aim of each mitzvah is to
benefit man, aside from the reward he receives from He who commanded it.

Our Sages have already said: "Why doesn't the Torah give reasons for the mitzvos? Because the reasons for two laws were revealed, and the great man of the world [Shlomoh] stumbled over
them . . ." [this proves there are reasons for the mitzvos].

[Another proof that there are reasons for the mitzvos is] the
Gemara in *Pesachim* 119b which expounds the verse, . . . *and for
the elegant clothing* (*Yeshayah* 23:18) as referring to one who un-
covers matters hidden by the Ancient of Days [G-d]. What are
these matters? The reasons for the commandments of the Torah.

The Rabbis, (Bamidbar Rabbah 19:3) expounding on the subject of the Red Cow, said: Shlomoh said: "I was able to understand the reasons for all the mitzvos, and I probed, researched, and delved into the chapter of the Red Cow, *I thought I could become wise, but it is beyond me* (*Koheles* 7:23). In that connection it says there: Rabbi Yose b. Rabbi Chanina said: The Holy One, blessed be He, said to Moshe: To you I reveal the reason for the Red Cow, but for everyone else it is a decree, as it says, *It will be on that day the light will not be very bright or very dim* (*Zechariah* 14:6). The word "or very dim" as written, reads "and will become revealed"—implying that matters concealed from you in this world will be revealed to you in the World to Come, like a blind man who begins to see, as it says, *I will lead the blind on a way they never knew . . . these are the things I shall have done and not have neglected them* (*Yeshayah* 42:16), for I have already done them to Rabbi Akiva, [for I have revealed the reason of the mitzvos to him].

The Rabbis explained that the reason we do not know the rationale of the commandments is because of our limited intellectual capacity, but the most obscure commandments have been revealed to the Jewish sages. The Rabbis have mentioned this very often, and it can be found in many sources in the Torah, and Tanach. The Rambam also mentions many of these sources.

The Mitzvos Are for Our Benefit

The Aggados[40] that the Rambam found difficult, [which seem to indicate that there are no reasons for the mitzvos], have a different meaning. I think they imply that the commandments do not benefit the Holy One, blessed be He, but do benefit man, protecting him from harm, evil beliefs, and vile character traits. Their purpose may be to remind us of the miracles and wonders of the Creator, so we know G-d. This is the intent of the above-mentioned Midrash (Bereishis Rabbah 44:1): "The only reason for the

---

40 ethical and inspirational teachings of the Talmud.

mitzvos is to refine people," so they become pure like refined silver. [The jeweler] who refines silver does not do so without purpose, rather he removes any impurity. So too, the mitzvos remove false beliefs from our hearts, showing us the truth and helping us remember it forever.

MITZVOS ARE GIVEN TO REFINE OUR CHARACTER

The above-cited Aggadah is also mentioned in *Tanchuma (Shemini 8)*: "What difference does it make to the Holy One, blessed be He, whether one eats an animal that was slaughtered through *shechitah* or piercing? Do you help Him or harm Him in any way? Or what difference does it make to Him whether you eat clean or unclean animals? But, *if you have become wise, you have become wise for your own good* (*Mishlei* 9:12). So you see, the only reason the mitzvos were given is to refine people, as it says, *The words of Hashem are pure words* (*Tehillim* 12:7), and, *Every word of G-d is refined* (*Mishlei* 30:5). Why? So that [His word] should protect you." End of the text of *Tanchuma*.

Here, the Rabbis explicitly tell us that the commandments were not given for the benefit of G-d, although one might think that the *Menorah* was made because G-d needs light, or that G-d needs the sacrifices for food or the burning of the incense for fragrance. Even the commandments to remember the miracles He performed at the Exodus and Creation were not given for G-d's benefit, rather so that we should know the truth and thereby be worthy of G-d's protection. Our veneration and our remembrance of His wonders mean nothing to Him.

[The law delineating] that slaughter must be done by cutting the front not the back of the neck or by piercing the animal proves that we, not G-d, benefit from the commandments. For it is impossible to say that the Creator derives more glory when *shechitah* is done from the throat rather than from the back of the neck, or by piercing the animal. Rather, the commandments were given for our benefit, to make us compassionate even when we slaughter the animal.

The Rabbis bring another proof: What difference does it make to G-d whether we eat pure animals—that is, permissible food, or impure animals—forbidden foods, about which the Torah says, *They are unclean to you* (*Vayikra* 11:26). They are only forbidden so we can attain a pure soul, becoming wise men who discern the truth.

MITZVOS PURIFY OUR SOULS

The Rabbis quoted the verse, *If you have become wise, you have become wise for your own good*, telling us that the commandments that define actions, such as *shechitah* by cutting the throat, are designed to teach us good character traits. The commandments delineating which animals [may be eaten] purify our souls, as the Torah says, *Do not make yourselves disgusting through animals, birds or anything that creeps on the ground that I have separated out for you as being unclean* (*Vayikra* 20:25). Therefore, all the commandments are solely for our benefit, as Elihu said, *If you have sinned, how have you affected Him? If your transgressions multiply, what have you done to Him? If you were righteous what have you given Him, or what has He taken from your hand?* (*Iyov* 35:6,7). All the Rabbis agree on this point.

And so they asked in *Yerushalmi* (*Nedarim* 9:1) whether it is permitted to suggest [to someone who made a vow] that G-d's honor will be affected in order to annul the vow[41] in a matter between man and G-d. The Rabbis explained there: "What is an example of a vow being annulled because of the honor of G-d?" [If you say to someone who vowed:] "I will not build a *sukkah*," or,

---

[41] If someone made a vow, is it permitted to suggest and say to him as a way to have his vow annulled: "Had you known that by making this vow you belittled G-d's honor?" If he says "yes," his vow may be annulled.

"I will not take the *lulav* in hand," or, "I will not put on *tefillin*," is that what you call: "affecting the honor due to G-d"? No, the one who performs the mitzvah derives the benefit! As it says, *If you were righteous what have you given Him, or what has He taken from your hand? If you have sinned, how have you affected Him? If your transgressions multiply, what have you done to Him?* End of the *Yerushalmi.*

Thus the Rabbis explain that even the [commandments of] *lulav, sukkah,* and *tefillin* which are *a sign on your arm and a reminder in the center of your head . . . for with a strong hand Hashem removed you from Egypt* (*Shemos* 13:9) were not given in honor of G-d, but out of compassion for our soul.

MITZVOS ARE GIVEN FOR OUR BENEFIT

The Rabbis put [this concept] into the words of the *Ne'ilah* prayer of Yom Kippur: "You set man apart from the beginning, and You considered Him worthy to stand before You, for who can tell You what to do, and if he is righteous what can he give You." And so it says in the Torah, *So that good will be yours* (*Devarim* 10:13). And further it says, *Hashem commanded you to keep all these rules, so that we would remain in awe of Hashem for all time for our good, so that we would survive* (6:24). The intent of all these verses is: [The mitzvos are given] for our good—not for His good. The purpose of all His commandments is for His creatures to be refined and purified from the dross of evil beliefs and contemptible character traits.

This is also the underlying thought of the Gemara in *Berachos* 33b: "If one says in his prayer: 'Your mercies extend even to a bird's nest,' he is silenced, because he suggests that the mitzvos of G-d are motivated by compassion, when in truth they are absolute decrees which we obey unquestioningly." The reason for the commandment of sending away the mother bird before taking the young, and prohibiting the slaughter of a cow and its calf on the same day is not because G-d had pity on them. His mercies on animals do not reach the point of preventing us from using them for our needs. Were that the case, G-d would forbid us to slaughter them. The reason for the prohibition [against taking the mother bird together with its young and slaughtering the cow and its calf on the same day] is to instill in us the trait of compassion, teaching us not to be cruel, because such acts tend to make a man cruel. Evidence of this is the fact that butchers who slaughter large oxen and donkeys are extremely vicious by nature. For this reason the Sages (Kiddushin 82a) said: "The worthiest of butchers is Amalek's partner."

To summarize: The reason for the commandments regarding cattle and fowl is not that G-d had compassion on the animals. They are decrees designed to educate us, about good character traits.

PRESERVING MORALITY ON THE BATTLEFIELD

23:10 **When you go out as a troop against your enemies, you must be on guard against anything evil.** Rashi comments: [Why specifically during wartime?] Because Satan accuses people in time of danger. End of Rashi's commentary.

I think this commandment warns us at a time when sin is unrestrained. Soldiers eat all kinds of loathsome things, rob and pillage, and are not ashamed of committing immorality and atrocities. Even decent people by nature become obsessed with cruelty and fury on the battlefield. Therefore the Torah warns us to *be on guard against anything*.

According the plain meaning of the verse, one should avoid everything forbidden. But *Sifrei* (23:16) says: I might think the passage refers to laws of uncleanness, purity and tithes. To teach you otherwise it says, *So that He will not see an* ervah, *shameful thing* (23:16) [which refers to sexual immorality]. From where do I know that idolatry, bloodshed, and blasphemy are included? From the

Torah verse, *You must be on guard against anything evil.* Perhaps
the verse includes even defilements, impurities, and tithes? To teach
you otherwise it says, *ervah,* "a shameful thing: just as *ervah* specifically refers to deeds for which the Canaanites were banished from
the Land, and which remove the *Shechinah* [from Yisrael], so too,
all deeds for which the Canaanites were driven from the Land and
which remove the *Shechinah* [from Yisrael] are included in the admonition of this verse. Since the Torah says, *ervas davar,* "a shameful thing," and the word "davar" also means speech we include
"evil talk" [gossip, and slander]. End of Sifrei commentary.

This fits our interpretation of the verse; in addition to the pro-
hibitions of these grave sins, a special prohibition to guard against
all these transgressions was added to the army, so the Shechinah
should not depart from Jewish soldiers. The Torah says, *"For
Hashem your G-d walks in the midst of your camp (23:16)"*, therefore, it says about one who commits these grave sins in the army
camp, *They have placed their abomination in the House upon which
My name is proclaimed, contaminating it (Yirmeyah 7:30)* [for they
cause the Shechinah to withdraw].

Another reason [to avoid these sins] is so enemies should not
defeat us, [for] if we commit the same deeds that caused them to
be driven out from before us, [we will have no reason to be treated differently.] This is the intent of the [end of the] verse, . . . *and
to grant you victory over your enemies (23:15).*

The Sages also included "evil speech" in this admonition so [the
soldiers] should not fight among themselves, causing more casualties than their enemies inflict on them.

MALICIOUS SPEECH AND SLANDER

24:9 **Remember what Hashem, your G-d, did to Miriam.**
Rashi comments: If you wish to avoid being stricken with
tzaraas, do not malign. [According to Rashi, this verse cautions
against evil speech but does not prohibit it].

In my opinion this is a positive commandment, like, *Remember the Shabbos day to keep it holy* (*Shemos* 20:8), and, *Remember this day, which you left Egypt* (13:3), and, *Remember what Amalek did to you* (*Devarim* 25:17), all of which are positive commandments. So too, "*Remember*" in the present verse, is a commandment forbidding slander. This commandment tells us to remember the severe punishment G-d gave the righteous prophetess, who spoke only about her brother who benefitted from her kindness (*Shemos* 2:7,8), and whom she loved as herself. She did not speak to his face so as not to embarrass him, but only in privacy to her brother [Aharon]. Yet her good deeds did not help her! So too, if *you sit and speak against your brother, you slander your mother's son* (*Tehillim* 50:20), you will not be saved [from punishment].

The *Sifrei* (Bechukosai) on the verse, *If you do not listen to Me and do not keep all these commandments* (*Vayikra* 26:14), comments: the verse, *and do not keep all these commandments,* refers to the commandments; what does, *If you do not listen to Me,* add? It includes working hard at learning the Torah. In the same vein, I might think the passage, *Remember the Shabbos day to keep it holy* (*Shemos* 20:8) means "remember it in your heart," however the verse, *Safeguard the Shabbos day to keep it holy* (*Devarim* 5:12) already teaches us to "safeguard it in our hearts"! We fulfill the mitzvah of *Remember,* by reciting it verbally. Similarly, it says, *Remember and never forget how you provoked Hashem, your G-d in the desert* (9:7). The phrase, *never forget* means "remember in your heart." How can one fulfill the mitzvah "to *remember*"? By reciting [this verse] verbally. Similarly, I might think, *Remember what Hashem your G-d did to Miriam,* means "remembering in the heart." But, *Be careful with regards to the* tzaraas *affliction, to be very careful and to act* (24:8), teaches us to remember in the heart! How can I fulfill "to *remember*"? By reciting [the commandment] verbally. Similarly, I might think, *Remember what Amalek did to you* (25:17) means "remember it in your heart." But the phrase, *Do not forget it* (25:19) refers to the heart! How can I fulfill *remember*? By verbally reciting [this section].

[But how can the verse, *Be careful with regard to the* tzaraas *af-*

fliction mean "retain in your heart what Hashem did to Miriam," because *Be careful with regard to the* tzaraas *affliction*, refers to tampering the tzaraas blemish after one was stricken]. The Sages interpreted the verse *Be careful with regard to* the tzaraas *affliction* to mean: *Beware of the* tzaraas *affliction*, being careful not to contract it [by remembering what G-d did to Miriam]. *And to do all that the Kohanim, the Levites teach you*, [not to cut away the physical symptoms of *tzaraas*]. Similarly, *Remember what Hashem, your G-d, did to Miriam*, means to always verbalize it.

The Rabbis consider this a commandment, not just a story and a recommendation on how to be saved from the plagues [as Rashi sees it]. Besides, how can slander which [the Sages (Arachin 15b) considered] as serious as murder not be forbidden in the Torah with an outright negative commandment, or at least a negative commandment derived from a positive commandment!

This verse contains a strict warning to refrain from slander publicly and privately, whether with intent to inflict harm or embarrass, or without intending any harm. This is one of the 613 mitzvos which the *Baal Halachos Gedolos* [the *Behag*] and others who counted the mitzvos forgot to include.

REMEMBERING AMALEK

25:17 **Remember what Amalek did to you . . .** I mentioned the exposition of *Sifrei* of the verse, *Remember what Amalek did to you*, above (24:9) stating: I might think it means "remember it in your heart." But the phrase, *Do not forget it* (25:19) refers to the heart! How can I fulfill the commandment to *remember*? By reciting it verbally. And *Sifrei* comments on the present verse: *Remember what Amalek did to you*—by reciting it verbally. *Do not forget it*—[but retain it] in your heart.

However, I do not know the intention of "remembering" through the spoken word. Perhaps it means reading the section on Amalek in the synagogue; if so from here we derive that reading *parashas Zachor*[42] is ordained by Torah law, and reading *Megillas Esther* [which relates the downfall of Haman, a descendant of Amalek] is also supported from the Torah.

In my opinion the correct interpretation of *Sifrei* is not to forget what Amalek did to us until his name is erased from under the heavens. We must relate this to our children and future generations, telling them: "This is what the wicked one did to us, and for this reason we are commanded to expunge his name."

THE EVIL OF *LESHON HARA*

Similarly, we are commanded to tell our children and future generations the episode of Miriam. Although it is proper to hide and not speak about the flaws of the righteous, the Torah commanded that [Miriam's failing] be revealed so the prohibition against malicious speech can be internalized. For [slander] is a grave sin, bringing many evils in its wake, and causing people to continuously stumble. As the Sages put it: "No one can avoid a slight suggestion of slander"(*Bava Basra* 165a).[43]

---

42 On *parashas Zachor* — Shabbos before Purim — after the reading of the weekly portion we read the section in *Devarim* (25:17-19) beginning with the word *Zachor*.

43 For example saying: "There is fire in the oven of so-and-so," suggesting that they are wealthy and eating all the time.

כי תבא

KI SAVO

—◈—

UPHOLDING THE TORAH

27:26 **Cursed is he who does not uphold and keep this entire Torah.**

Rashi comments: Here [Moshe] included the entire Torah, and they accepted it upon themselves with a curse and an oath. End of Rashi's commentary.

In my opinion, "upholding and keeping the Torah" means affirming the commandments in one's heart, considering them as truth, and believing that whoever observes them will be rewarded with goodness, and whoever violates them will be punished. If one denies the validity of even one commandment, or thinks one of them has been revoked permanently, he is cursed. But if one transgresses one of the commandments, such as eating pork or some detestable creature out of desire, or not building a *sukkah* or taking the *lulav* in hand out of laziness, he is not cursed; for the Torah does not say, "who does not perform this entire Torah," but rather, *who does not uphold and keep this entire Torah*, as in the phrase, *The Jews confirmed and undertook upon themselves* (*Esther* 9:27). Thus the curse in our verse is directed at people who rebel [against the Torah] denying [its truth].

The *Yerushalmi* (Sotah 7:4), comments on the verse, *He who does not uphold*—Is the Torah about to fall down [that it needs to be upheld?] Rabbi Shimon ben Yakim says: This refers to a sexton who does not stand the Torah scrolls properly in the Ark. Rabbi Shimon ben Chalafta says: This refers to a court [which fails to use its power to influence transgressors to observe the Torah.] For Rav Yehudah and Rav Huna said in the name of Shmuel: When [King] Yoshiahu heard this verse he rent his garments, saying: "It is my duty to raise up [the Torah]." Rabbi Assi said in the name of Rabbi Tanchum bar Chiya: If someone learned and taught Torah, observed and performed [the mitzvos], and had the means to [influence others to] uphold the Torah but did not, he is included among those that are cursed. End of the *Yerushalmi*.

BRINGING OTHERS CLOSER TO TORAH

The *Yerushalmi* demands that kings and leaders uphold the Torah, for they have power to influence those who seek to destroy the Torah. Even a perfectly righteous individual who is capable of influencing evildoers [to become loyal to the Torah but fails to do so], is cursed. This is similar to the way we explained the verse.

HAGBAHAH, RAISING THE TORAH ALOFT

The Rabbis [of this *Yerushalmi*] as an Aggadic explanation, said this refers to a sexton who fails to stand the Torah scrolls properly so they do not fall. I think this refers to the sexton who fails to raise the Torah scroll showing the writing to the congregation. It says in *Maseches Soferim* (14:14) that one should lift the Torah scroll, showing the written side to the people standing at his right and left, turning forward and backward, because it is a mitzvah for all the men and women to see the writing, bowing down and saying, *This is the Torah that Moshe placed before B'nei Yisrael*, as is our custom.

THE TOCHACHAH—ADMONITION

28:15-69 And it will be if you do not listen to the voice of Hashem your G-d to guard to do all His commandments and statutes which I command you today, and all these curse shall come upon you . . .

The warnings of misfortune, confusion, frustration, pestilence, blight of the trees and fruits of the land, and the other admonitions [mentioned in this portion], refer to the period before the Jews were driven out of Eretz Yisrael. The only evil [Moshe] predicts regarding [the exile] following the expulsion, is that *there you will serve idolaters who worship wood and stone* (28:36). At times he backtracks warning them of [things that will happen] while they are still in the Land, for example, *Hashem will bring you and your elected king to a nation unknown to you and your father, and there you will serve idolaters . . .* (28:36), referring to the exile to Rome, because King Agrippas traveled to Rome. Afterwards [Moshe] returns [to an earlier period] saying, *You will bring much seed out to the field, but the locusts will devour [the crop] . . .* (28:38), referring to the time when they are still in the Land; later he says, *You will be torn up from the Land* (28:63), referring to the exile again. In my opinion, Moshe, hinting at future events says, *Hashem will bring you and your elected king to a nation unknown to you* (28:36), alluding to King Agrippa's journey to Rome [and not to the Roman exile].

It is possible that Moshe is alluding to Aristobulus, the king who reigned before Agrippa, who was captured by a Roman general and taken to Rome in copper chains where he became *a byword and a conversation piece among all the nations* (28:37). They used to be amazed at the valor of the Jews, [and now exclaim:] "How the mighty have fallen and the weapons of war gone to waste!"

[Much later Agrippa's son,] Agrippa II came once again to Eretz Yisrael with an emissary of the Roman emperor, capturing large cities in Judea, in fulfillment of Moshe's prophecy, *You will serve your enemies when Hashem sends them against you, and you will be in hunger, thirst, nakedness and universal want* (28:48).

Moshe continued, *Hashem will bring upon you a nation from afar* (28:49), for Vespasian and his son Titus came to Eretz Yisrael with a vast Roman legion, capturing all the fortified cities in Judea and oppressing them harshly, as recorded in history books. They also captured the walls of Yerushalayim; only the Beis Hamikdash and the wall of the Courtyard were left standing. [Starving] people ate the flesh of their sons and daughters. And when [the Beis Hamikdash] was captured, the prophecy of, *You will be torn up from the land* (28:63) came true. The Romans returned to their country taking the exiles of Yerushalayim with them. Following the example of the Romans, other nations including Greece, Egypt and Syria exiled Jews into their land, fulfilling the prophecy, *Hashem will scatter you among the nations* (28:64).

The suffering is described in the subsequent verses which refer to the exile, such as, *Your life will hang by a thread before you* (28:66), because in exile we live in fear of the nations who constantly issue decrees against us.

This verse alludes to the generations that lived during the era of the destruction of the second Beis Hamikdash, when the Romans plotted to exterminate the Jews completely. The next verse, *Hashem will bring you back to Egypt in ships* (28:68), happened when the Romans finished expelling the Jews from the Land.

Our Rabbis comment on this: "Why were they brought back to Egypt? Because it is utterly repugnant for a servant to be forced to return to his former master." Therefore Moshe mentions Egypt as an admonishment.

PROMISE OF REDEMPTION

However, the products we manufacture in exile in the lands of our enemies have not been cursed. Neither have the calves of our herds, the lambs of our flock, our vineyards, our olive trees, and the seeds we have sown [been damaged]. Rather, we live in the lands of the exile, like or better than, the local population, because

G-d has been compassionate with us. Our existence in exile is made possible by the promise G-d made to us, *Thus, even when they are in their enemies' land, I will not grow disgusted with them nor tired of them that I would destroy them and break My covenant with them, for I am Hashem, their G-d* (*Vayikra* 26:44)

I have already explained in *parashas Bechukosai* (*Vayikra* 26:16), that this covenant refers to the era of our present exile where we are under the domination of "the fourth beast" [in the prophecy of *Daniel* 7:7] representing Rome. Moshe promises that the complete redemption [from our *galus*,] will come afterwards saying, *Hashem will bring back your remnants and have mercy on you. Hashem your G-d will gather you from where He scattered you. Even if your diaspora is at the ends of the heavens, Hashem your G-d will gather you up from there and He will take you back* (30:3).

נצבים

NITZAVIM

———◆———

FREEDOM OF CHOICE BETWEEN GOOD AND EVIL

30:6 Hashem will circumcise your heart and the heart of your offspring to love Hashem . . .

Our Sages said about this: "If you come to purify yourself, you will be helped from Above." In this verse G-d promises He will help one who returns to Him with all his heart.

Ever since Creation man has had freedom to choose to be righteous or wicked. Throughout the era of the Torah, man retains this freedom of choice in order to earn reward for making the right choice and to be punished for making the wrong one. But with the coming of Mashiach, choosing to do good will come naturally. Man will have no desire to do the unacceptable, and evil will hold no allure for him.

This is the "circumcision" of which our verse speaks. Desire and craving are the "foreskin" of the heart. Circumcising one's heart means excising lust and desire. In the days of Mashiach man will return to the mindset of Adam before he sinned, when he instinctively did what should be done and had no [need for] freedom to choose between good and evil, as I explained in *parashas Bereishis* (2:9).

This idea is expressed in the verse, *Behold days are coming—the word of Hashem—when I will seal a new covenant with the House of*

*Yisrael and with the House of Yehudah; not like the covenant I sealed
with their forefathers* . . . *For this is the covenant that I shall seal with
the House of Yisrael after those days—the word of Hashem—I will
place My Torah within them and I will write it onto their heart* . . .
(*Yirmeyah* 31:30-32). Yirmeyah meant the elimination of the evil
impulse, when the heart intuitively does the right thing.

Therefore the verse continues, *I will be a G-d for them, and they
will be a people for Me. They will no longer teach—each man his fel-
low, each man his brother—saying "Know Hashem!" For all of them
will know Me, from their smallest to their greatest* (32,33). Now, *the
imagery of man's heart is evil from his youth* (*Bereishis* 8:21), and
man must be taught [how to subdue his evil impulse], but then, it
will not be necessary to teach him, because the evil impulse will be
gone completely.

Yechezkel said, *I will give you a new heart and put a new spirit
within you; I will remove the heart of stone from your flesh and give
you a heart of flesh* . . . *and I will make it so that you will follow My
decrees and guard My ordinances and fulfill them* (*Yechezkel*
36:26,27). The "new heart" refers to man's nature, and the "new
spirit" signifies his desire and will. Accordingly the Rabbis
(Shabbos 151b) expounded on the verse, *And those years arrive of
which you will say, "I have no pleasure in them"* (*Koheles* 12:1)—
"this refers to the days of Mashiach when there will be neither
merit nor guilt." Because man will no longer have a desire [to do
evil]; rather he will instinctively do the right thing, he will have no
merit or guilt, because merit and guilt are dependent on desire.

הַאֲזִינוּ
HA'AZINU

———◦◉◦———

G-D WILL NOT ALLOW YISRAEL'S DESTRUCTION

32:26 I said I will become angry with them, I will make their memory vanish from among mankind, were it not that the anger of the enemy was pent up.

This is a reference to our current exile among the nations. We are the offspring of the tribes of Yehudah and Binyamin,[44] yet in the eyes of the nations we are not even worth mentioning; we are not considered a people at all. According to the Divine attribute of Justice we should remain in exile forever, *were it not that the anger of the enemy was pent up* (32:27). In our present exile the merit of the Patriarchs has been exhausted[45] [and, we can no longer rely on that protection]; we have no possibility of being rescued from the hands of our enemies except for the sake of His great Name, as the *navi* Yechezkel says, *When I remove you from the peoples and gather you from the lands where you were scattered, and I will be sanctified through you in the eyes of the nations. Then you will know that I am Hashem, when I act with you for My Name's sake, and not in accord with your evil ways and your corrupt deeds, by which you became de-*

---

44 All Jews living today are descended of the tribes of Levi, Yehudah and Binyamin. The other ten tribes are lost.

45 according to Shmuel in *Shabbos* 55a.

filed, O House of Yisrael! (*Yechezkel* 20:41,44), and furthermore it
says, *But I acted for the sake of My name, that I not be desecrated in
the eyes of the nations* (20:9).

YISRAEL, G-D'S ONLY FAITHFUL SERVANT

[Since our deliverance from the nations is only for the sake of
His great Name,] Moshe said in his prayer [on behalf of Yisrael
after the return of the spies], *Now You want to kill this entire nation like a single man! The nations who hear this news about You will
say, "Hashem was not able to bring this nation to the land"*
(*Bamidbar* 14:15). And G-d accepted his plea, replying, *I will
grant forgiveness as you have requested* (14:20).

This does not mean G-d wanted to show His strength to His enemies, *for all the nations together are like nothing before Him, as noth-
ingness and emptiness are they reckoned by Him* (*Yeshayah* 40:17)

It means: G-d created man so he can know G-d is the Creator,
and be thankful to His Name. He gave man the freedom to choose
to do evil or good. All the nations sinned denying His existence,
and only [the Jewish] people remained His loyal servant, so He
made known through them, by signs and wonders, that He is the
G-d of gods and the L-rd of lords. That is how He became known
to all the nations.

In light of this, were Yisrael to cease existing, the nations would
forget G-d's wonders and deeds, no longer talking about them.
Were someone to mention [G-d's miracles], they would think it
was done through the power of the constellations and stars, and
[the knowledge of G-d's wonders] would vanish and be forgotten.
Should that happen, the purpose of the creation of man would be
undermined completely. No one who knows his Creator would be
left; only people who infuriate Him would remain.

For the sake of the creation of the world, G-d wants to preserve
the Jewish people as His nation forever. They are nearer to Him
and know Him better than all other nations.

That is the underlying thought of the verse, *When Hashem will have judged His people, He shall relent regarding His servants* (32:36). G-d in His mercy will remember that the Jews have been His people since time immemorial. He will recall that they are His servants who remained faithful to him in their exile, suffering anguish and bondage, as it says, *But they are My nation sons who do not lie.* I have already hinted at the deep secret of the purpose of being a nation for Him, and for Him being our G-d. As it says, *Everyone whom I have created for My Name and whom I have created for My glory* (*Yeshayah* 63:8).

PREDICTION OF THE COMING REDEMPTION

33:40 This Song, our true and faithful testimony, tells us clearly what will happen to us. It begins with G-d's kindness in making us His portion (32:8,9). Then it relates the favors He granted us in the wilderness (32:10-12), giving us the lands of great and mighty nations and the abundance of goodness and wealth in [those lands]. But when there was plenty of everything they rebelled against Him, worshipping idols (32:16-18). The Song then describes G-d's anger [with Yisrael], (32:19-22) bringing plague, famine, predatory beasts, and invaders to their land (32:23-25), followed by dispersion all over the world (32:26). Clearly, all this has come true to the letter.

The Song then predicts (32:41) that ultimately, G-d will bring vengeance on His enemies and repay those who hated Him. They [deserve to be punished] because they brought all these evils on us out of hatred of the Holy One, blessed be He. They hated the Jews because they did not become like them, [for the Jews] worshipped G-d, fulfilled His commandments, did not intermarry with them, did not eat their slaughtered [animals], held their idols in contempt, and uprooted their idols, as it says, *Because of Your sake we are killed all the time* (*Tehillim* 44:23). Thus they abuse us because they hate the Holy One, blessed be He. They are G-d's enemies, and He rightfully takes revenge against them.

[The Song ends, *O nations, sing the praises of the people.* . . . *He will bring vengeance upon His foes, and reconcile His land and His people* (32:43).]

It is clear that in this Song, G-d refers to the future redemption. [It cannot refer to the era of the second Beis Hamikdash,] because during the construction of the second Beis Hamikdash, the nations did not *sing the praises of His people.* Instead, they taunted them, saying, *What are these Jewish weaklings doing?* (*Nechemiah* 3:34), and their leaders [Daniel, Chananiah, Mishael, and Azariah] were servants in the palace of the king of Babylonia, and all the Jews were subservient to him. In those days G-d did not *take revenge against His enemies, and He did not reconcile His land and His people.*

The Song does not make the future redemption conditional on repentance. Rather, it is a declaration predicting that we will transgress, and that in His anger G-d will punish us, but we will not be totally obliterated. He will relent and pay back His enemies with His harsh, great, and mighty sword, and forgive our sins for His name's sake.

This Song is a promise of the future redemption, despite the Christians words. The Rabbis mentioned in *Sifrei*: Great is this Song because it speaks of the present, the past, and the future; it speaks of this world and of the World to Come.

This is hinted at in the following verse, *Moshe came and proclaimed all the words of this Song to the people* (32:44). "*All the words*" teach us that, although it is a brief statement it contains all the events that will happen to the Jewish people in the future, for Moshe explained all its implications.

Had a gentile prophet written this Song, foretelling the future, he would deserve belief, for it has been fulfilled in every detail up to now. Surely, therefore, we should look forward to the fulfillment of the word of G-d through His prophet Moshe, the trusted servant throughout His house. Before him there was no one like him, and nor was there after him.

וזאת הברכה
VEZOS HABERACHAH

―――◆―――

THE TWELVE TRIBES

33:6 **May Reuven live and not die** . . . Rabbi Avraham ibn Ezra explains that Moshe began with Reuven because he is the first-born. He does not mention Shimon because of the sin of Pe'or,[46] for all those who worshipped [Baal Pe'or] were from the tribe of Shimon. Their [smaller] number [at the second tally] proves this [because 24,000 of them died in the plague after the sin]. Their prince [Zimri ben Salu] was also killed in the wake of the episode. Rashi and other commentators share ibn Ezra's view.

. . . In my opinion, the Torah always counts the tribes of Yisrael as only twelve. So it says in Yaakov's blessing, *All these are the tribes of Yisrael, twelve in all* (*Bereishis* 49:28). Yaakov mentioned his twelve sons, counting Yosef as one tribe (49:22-26) [rather than counting Efraim and Menasheh]. But Moshe preferred to mention Yosef as two tribes, as he said, *They are the myriad of Efraim and the thousands of Menasheh* (33:17). He did this for two reasons:

Firstly, the Holy One, blessed be He, commanded that [Efraim and Menasheh] be considered as two tribes at the dedication of the Altar (*Bamidbar* 7:48 and 54), the banners [i.e., the placement of the tribes around the Tabernacle in the wilderness] (2:18,21)], and

---

46 The women of Moav enticed the Jews to immorality and to worshipping Baal Pe'or (*Bamidbar* 25:1-9).

the distribution of the inheritance of the Land (34:23,24). Therefore, Moshe counted them as two tribes.

Secondly, since he mentioned that Yehoshua would take possession of the Land [on behalf of the people], and Yehoshua was from the tribe of Efraim, the younger son [of Yosef], he had to mention Menasheh, the older son.

WHY MOSHE DID NOT BLESS SHIMON

Moshe wanted to bless the tribe of Levi, because through [Levi's] blessing all Yisrael would be blessed that their offerings be favorably accepted by G-d. Therefore, he had to omit one of the other tribes, for no more than twelve tribes are counted in all of the Torah, matching the twelve constellations of the zodiac, the twelve months of the year, . . . as the Rabbis (Berachos 32b.) said: The Holy One, blessed be He, said to the prophet: "Go, tell the community of Yisrael: My daughter, I have created twelve constellations in the sky to correspond to the twelve tribes."

Similarly, at Mount Gerizim and Mount Eival when the Torah mentions the tribe of Levi (*Devarim* 26:12), Yosef is not counted as two tribes [and therefore Shimon is mentioned]. By the apportioning of the Land (*Yechezkel* 48:4,5) where Yosef is counted as two tribes, Levi is not mentioned (*Yechezkel* 48:4,5). When Yechezkel counts the gates of Yerushalayim he mentions *the gate of Levi* (48:31), and does not count Yosef as two tribes. Instead he says, *The gate of Yosef, one* (48:32), because the tribes of Yisrael are never counted as more than twelve. I mentioned this already in *parashas Korach* (17:17).

Therefore Moshe omitted Shimon [from his blessings]. The tribe of Shimon was not large, for G-d did not mean to bless Shimon with burgeoning population. Instead he dispersed [Shimon and Levi] in Yaakov and scattered them among Yisrael (*Bereishis* 49:7). Thus they too were blessed by the blessing of the other tribes among whom they lived . . .

אחרית דבר
CONCLUSION

———◦◉◦———

The five books are now completed,

Which even Shlomoh's wisdom was insufficient to compre-
hend.

Blessing and thanksgiving to G-d,

Who did me good with mercy and abundant kindness,

And granted me my heart's desire.

May He be willing for His Name's sake,

That the Redeemer shall come to Zion,

That speedily in our days Michael may arise,

And build the Beis Hamikdash and the Altar.

May the verse written by Yechezkel be fulfilled:

Then the nations will know that I am Hashem

Who sanctifies Yisrael,

When My sanctuary will be among them forever

Blessed Be Hashem the G-d of Yisrael forever,

From this world to the World to Come, You are G-d.

Amen and Amen

GLOSSARY

B'NEI YISRAEL - Children of Israel
BAMIDBAR - The Book of Numbers
BEIS HAMIKDASH - Holy Temple
BEREISHIS - The Book of Genesis
CHAZZAN - leader of the prayer service
DEVARIM - The Book of Deuteronomy
DIVREI HAYAMIM - The Book of Chronicles
EICHA - The Book of Lamentations
ERETZ YISRAEL - The Land of Israel
GALUS - exile
GEMARA - Talmud
HASHEM - God
IYOV - Job
KIDDUSH - a declaration sanctifying the beginning of a holy day
KOHEIN pl. *KOHANIM* - Priests, descendants of Aaron
KOHELES - Ecclesiastes
MASHIACH - The Messiah
MELACHIM - The Book of Kings
MISHLEI - Proverbs
MITZVAH pl. *MITZVOS* - commandment
PARASHAS - the portion [of the Torah]
SANHEDRIN - Jewish High Court
SHABBOS - The day of rest - Saturday
SHECHINA - Divine Presence
SHEMOS - The Book of Exodus
SHIR HASHIRIM - Song of Songs
SHMUEL - The Book of Samuel
SHOFAR - Ram's horn blown on Rosh Hashana
SHOFTIM - The Book of Judges
SUKKAH - hut used on Tabernacles
TEFILLIN - phylacteries
TEHILLIM Psalms
TZITZIS - fringes worn on a four cornered garment
VAYIKRA - The Book of Leviticus
YAAKOV - Jacob
YERUSHALAYIM - Jerusalem
YESHAYAH - Isaiah
YIRMIYAH - Jeremiah
YISRAEL - Israel

118